C000150587

DEAR MISS WALKER

GALLIPOLI, EGYPT AND PALESTINE, FRANCE
1915-18

Wartime Letters from Distant Fronts

Edited by Toddy Hoare

Helion & Company

Helion & Company Limited
Unit 8 Amherst Business Centre
Budbrooke Road
Warwick
CV34 5WE
England
Tel. 01926 499 619
Fax 0121 711 4075
Email: info@helion.co.uk
Website: www.helion.co.uk
Twitter: @helionbooks
Visit our blog http://blog.helion.co.uk/

Published by Helion & Company 2018
Designed and typeset by Farr out Publications, Wokingham
Cover designed by Paul Hewitt, Battlefield Design (www.battlefield-design.co.uk)
Printed by Hobbs The Printers Ltd, Totton, Hampshire

Text © Toddy Hoare 2018
Images from the editor's collection unless credited otherwise
Maps drawn by George Anderson © Helion & Company 2018

Front cover: Yeomanry charging Ottoman infantry which attacked with bayonets owing to
their ammunition failing. (*Illustrated London News*, 16 February 1918)

Every reasonable effort has been made to trace copyright holders and to obtain their permission
for the use of copyright material. The author and publisher apologize for any errors or omissions
in this work and would be grateful if notified of any corrections that should be incorporated in
future reprints or editions of this book.

ISBN 978-1-910777-19-0

British Library Cataloguing-in-Publication Data
A catalogue record for this book is available from the British Library.

All rights reserved. No part of this publication may be reproduced, stored in a retrieval system,
or transmitted, in any form, or by any means, electronic, mechanical, photocopying, recording
or otherwise, without the express written consent of Helion & Company Limited.

For details of other military history titles published by Helion & Company Limited contact the
above address or visit our website: http://www.helion.co.uk.

We always welcome receipt of book proposals from prospective authors.

Contents

List of Illustrations

List of Maps

Abbreviations

ADC: Aide de Camp. Assistant to a more senior officer.

Army: Largest fighting formation comprised of two or more corps commanded by a full general.

BAOR: British Army of the Rhine, post-1945 military occupation of West Germany.

Battalion, Regiment: Basic army unit, battalion being Infantry, regiment most others.

Bgd./Bde: Brigade: Fighting unit made up of a number of teeth arm regiments and supporting units.

C -in- C: Commander in Chief.

CO: Commanding Officer usually of a regiment and above.

OC: Officer Commanding. Senior officer commanding any unit.

Col. Colonel: Usually a regimental CO is a Lieutenant-Colonel, while a full colonel is the junior rank of senior staff having progressed beyond regimental duties. An Honorary Colonel is the traditional Colonel of a regiment with no duties in the field but with an overall care for the regiment, often linked to recruiting or interviewing new officers. Colonel-in-Chief is a senior Hon. Col. with no regimental duties bar formal or parade inspections and is usually a member of the Royal Family.

Teeth Arms: The basic fighting units of the army: Cavalry, Infantry, etc., etc.

Corps: Formation comprising a number of Divisions. Commanded by a Lieutenant General.

Division: a fighting formation made up of a number of Brigades and supporting units. Commanded by a Major-General.

DSO: Distinguished Service Order, in recognition of duties performed but not necessarily with weapon in hand.

GOC: General Officer Commanding a division and above.

MC: Military Cross, for gallantry performing duties in the field. (Not a posthumous award.)

Mess: Where soldiers ate together from latin Misso where a portion is sent (Mess) out. Thus, where NCOs and Officers respectively gathered to live and eat.

MG: Machine gun.

NCO: Non-Commissioned Officer, anyone ranking above a Trooper (Cavalry) or Guardsman/Private (Infantry) but below a Warrant Officer.

RAC: Royal Armoured Corps which comprises all cavalry and tank regiments.

S/H: Spot height.

Sqn: Squadron, Cavalry regiments usually has three squadrons commanded by majors of four troops of 12 men each commanded by a Troop Leader. A 4th sqn was HQ Sqn.

Warrant Officer: senior other rank below officers holding a Warrant rather than a Commission.

Yeo: Yeomanry, erritorial Mounted County Regiment, with personnel normally providing personnel horses for which they were reimbursed.

Foreword

This book presents a series of 82 letters written by Brigadier-General Reginald Hoare (1865-1947) during the First World War. They allow us to explore a number of different themes. Firstly, Hoare's experiences remind us that this was a global war. Secondly, the book offers valuable insight into several aspects of army life. Here we have a range of detail on the variety of theatres in which British troops were asked to fight, and on issues such as officer-man relations and the maintenance of morale; and a window that allows us to glimpse 'the face of battle'. Perhaps just as striking, though, are the long passages in which there was *no* battle: a reminder that the daily experience of the soldier was often one of training, recreation, or boredom, rather than fighting. Finally, through these letters we see two people whose lives were put on hold by war: from the first 'Dear Miss Walker' letter to their wedding day on October 1918 was a period of over three years, during which Hoare's first priority was to get the job done.

Hoare's wartime career spanned three continents. In common with many soldiers of his generation, he had fought in the South African War (1899-1902), and his experience made him valuable in 1914-15 as the British army expanded to fight a Continental war. During the first months of the war he trained the 2nd Mounted Division, which was sent to Gallipoli. By December 1914, deadlock seemed to have set in on the Western Front, and many now began to question whether or not success could be achieved in an 'alternative and easier theatre'.[1] An attack on the Ottoman Empire, which joined the Central Powers at the end of October 1914, seemed to provide an opportunity to knock a German ally out of the war, open up a route to Russia, and ultimately strike at the 'soft underbelly' of the Central Powers. However, the naval assault on the Dardanelles, which began on 19 February 1915, was a failure. Troops were landed on 25 April, but were soon bogged down on the Gallipoli Peninsula. The ability of the 'sick man of Europe' to withstand assault was widely underestimated.[2] 'I wonder if we shall be in Constantinople before Xmas', wrote Hoare on 14 September (letter 2), ahead of his departure. However, by the time he arrived in theatre, realistic hopes to push on at Gallipoli had long vanished. This would not be the last time Hoare would be confronted by the stubbornness of Ottoman troops on the defensive. As winter approached, the question of whether Britain should continue to support a force on the peninsula grew more urgent. This was compounded when a heavy storm struck in

---

1   C.F. Aspinall-Oglander, *History of the Great War, Military Operations: Gallipoli*, Vol I (London: William Heinemann, 1929), p. 44. On the Gallipoli campaign, see also C.F. Aspinall-Oglander, *History of the Great War, Military Operations: Gallipoli*, Vol II (London: William Heinemann, 1932); Rhys Crawley and Michael LoCicero, *Gallipoli: New Perspectives on the Mediterranean Expeditionary Force, 1915-16* (Solihull: Helion, 2018); Christopher M. Bell, *Churchill and the Dardanelles* (Oxford: Oxford University Press, 2017); Peter Hart, *Gallipoli* (London: Profile, 2011); Robin Prior, *Gallipoli: The End of the Myth* (London: Yale University Press, 2009); Tim Travers, *Gallipoli 1915* (Stroud: Tempus, 2001); Les Carlyon, *Gallipoli* (Australia: Pan Macmillan Australia, 2001); Michael Hickey, *Gallipoli* (London: John Murray, 1998). For a good summary of historiography prior to 1991, see Edward Spiers, 'Gallipoli', in Bond (ed.), *The First World War*, pp. 165-188.

2   David French, 'The Origins of the Dardanelles Campaign Reconsidered', *History*, 68: 223 (1983), pp. 210-224.

November: 'The conditions for the men in the trenches were most trying', Hoare wrote (letter 4). On 7 December, the Cabinet finally decided to evacuate the Anzac and Suvla, and Helles was duly evacuated on the night of 8-9 January 1916. Both evacuations were accomplished with almost no casualties; 'we outwitted and completely hoodwinked the Turks', Hoare wrote, 'and got away from the Peninsular without their ever knowing we were going, till we were gone' (letter 5).

Hoare's next stop was Egypt. Egypt had effectively been a part of the British Empire since 1882, although Ottoman suzerainty was retained until 1914. Ottoman entry into the war finally prompted Britain to end the fiction of Ottoman control by declaring Egypt a Protectorate. The British were sensitive about Egypt for a number of reasons. Chief among these was the Suez Canal, a vital link in the chain of British maritime communications. Egypt also served as a base for the Gallipoli and Salonika expeditions – although these drained it of men and resources – and it ultimately became something of a general reserve for the Empire. The point about Egypt's military importance is made clear by the fact that by the end of 1915 it was supporting a total of four fronts: Gallipoli, Salonika, against Ottoman forces on the Suez Canal, and against a rising of the Senussi in the Western desert. There was also concern that any of these could touch off fighting on a fifth front: namely, an internal rising of the Egyptian population.

After a period back in Britain, Hoare joined the Egyptian Expeditionary Force (EEF) in summer 1916: it was unsettling to be sent back, he noted, 'but war is unsettling, isn't it?' (letter 14). With the 2nd Dismounted Brigade he was responsible for '300 miles of the Western frontier' (letter 16). Hoare was involved in operations against the Senussi, not without success: on 31 October, he reported capturing 196 Senussi fighters (letter 22). The campaign was largely concluded by the end of 1916. As Hoare put it, on 20 December, 'the Senusi are very quiet now, and I think have found that fighting doesn't pay' (letter 25).[3]

Following the defeat of the second Ottoman offensive in mid-1916, thoughts began to turn to the attack as the EEF took the initiative. The Ottoman Empire was increasingly feeling the strain by 1917. Baghdad fell on 11 March 1917, and Hoare expected the Empire to sue for a separate peace (letter 30). He certainly knew what was at stake: his letter of 5 April is signed '60 miles from Jerusalem' (letter 31). However, the defeat of Ottoman forces would require hard fighting. The EEF, commanded by General Sir Archibald Murray, launched its offensive in the spring. In the First and Second Battles of Gaza (26 March and 17-19 April), Murray's attacks were repulsed. 'We keep hammering away at the Turks', Hoare wrote on 20 June, and although he noted a prisoner's claim that many more wanted to surrender, he was somewhat sceptical (letter 34).

Murray was replaced by General Edmund Allenby, and an operational pause followed. Allenby launched his attack on 31 October (the Battle of Beersheba). Allenby's offensive succeeded and drove the Ottomans back; they fought a number of rearguard actions, but were unable to establish a coherent defensive position or push the EEF back. Hoare believed that the EEF had 'got the Turks on the run' (letter 42) and wrote on 26 November that he hoped Jerusalem would fall (letter 43). Indeed, the fall of the city on 9 December was a significant victory for the EEF, and also a major blow to the Ottoman Empire. The Palestine

---

3   For operations against the Senussi, see George MacMunn and Cyril Falls, *Military Operations Egypt & Palestine*, Vol I (London: HMSO, 1928).

campaign brought four centuries of Ottoman rule in the region to an end.[4]

On 21 March 1918, the Germans launched an offensive on the Western Front which aimed at achieving a knock-out blow. Allenby's campaign entered a period of stalemate as thousands of troops were sent to the Western Front. Hoare was one of them. For the first time, he found himself facing the German army. 'In a way I am rather sorry to have left the other country we came from, as I should have liked to have seen the campaign out there', he wrote on 19 May of his move from Palestine. 'On the other hand, it's nice to be nearer home in Europe once more, and after all this is the main show – the other was a "side show"' (letter 52). The German offensives failed, taking a lot of extra territory but without knocking Britain out of the war, defeating the French army, or taking Paris. The pendulum swung during the Second Battle of the Marne, which began on 15 July. On 18 July, the French launched a major counter-attack, a success which Hoare notes (letter 55). Thereafter, the initiative rested with the Allies. During the Hundred Days (8 August – 11 November), Allied offensives pushed the Germans back. 'We are still moving on chasing the retreating Bosch, & all goes well', Hoare wrote on 7 September (letter 67). It was during this advance that Hoare was wounded by a shell (letter 68), giving him a 'nice comfortable wound' that allowed him to go back to Britain (letter 70).[5]

Hoare's war is also interesting because of his observations of the places to which he travelled, and what his letters tell us about the day-to-day experience of war. When in Egypt and Palestine, he repeatedly comments on the heat; and his letters are filled with descriptions of the country. 'In spite of the heat the men have kept wonderfully well', he wrote on 24 August 1916, and sport and music played an important role in maintaining spirits (letter 19). On the other hand, he also comments on periods of boredom: 'Here our life has lately been uneventful, and without excitement', he wrote on 10 February 1917 (letter 28). The war in Egypt and Palestine was very much a 'campaign against nature'; sickness was a key consideration here, and Hoare talks of fighting flies and scorpions (letter 32). Time was also spent in preparation, and the pause in operations in mid-1917 allowed time for 'training our men how to defeat "Johnny" Turk' (letter 37). Hoare writes of his experiences of battle, including trench-building operations and raids. On the Western Front, he was struck by the level of devastation wrought by industrial war (letters 59 and 64) and by the effects of German shelling, including gas (letter 59). Finally, the 'love letters' (Hoare's own description!) at the end of the collection reveal the difficulties of separation and remind us of the continued importance of the domestic sphere to men in the trenches.

Hoare's war therefore offers a useful perspective on the First World War. He trained up to fight the German army, but then spent most of the years 1915-18 fighting the Ottoman

---

4   On the Palestine campaign, see MacMunn Falls, *Military Operations Egypt & Palestine*, Vol I; Cyril Falls, *Military Operations Egypt & Palestine*, Vol II (London: HMSO, 1930); Matthew Hughes, *Allenby and British Strategy in the Middle East, 1917-1919* (Abingdon: Frank Cass, 1999); James Kitchen, *The British Imperial Army in the Middle East: Morale and Military Identity in the Sinai and Palestine Campaigns, 1916-18* (London: Bloomsbury, 2014).

5   On the Western Front in 1918, see James Edmonds, *Military Operations France and Belgium, 1918*, 5 vols. (London: HMSO, 1935-47); David Stevenson, *With Our Backs to the Wall: Victory and Defeat in 1918* (London: Allen Lane, 2011); David Zabecki, *The German 1918 Offensives: A Case Study in the Operational Level of War* (Abingdon: Routledge, 2006); J.P. Harris and Niall Barr, *Amiens to the Armistice: The BEF in the Hundred Days* (London: Brassey's, 1998); Jonathan Boff, *Winning and Losing on the Western Front* (Cambridge: Cambridge University Press, 2012); Nick Lloyd, *Hundred Days: The End of the Great War* (London: Penguin, 2013).

army and the Senussi. He was sent to the Western Front at the height of Britain's greatest crisis of the war, before participating in the army's victorious advance. The letters that follow represent the story of a world at war, through one man's eyes.

Daniel Whittingham PhD
Birmingham
September 2018

Acknowledgements

I must thank my cousin Nicholas Hoare, also known as Reg since Eton where there was more than one Nicholas Hoare, for rescuing Grandpa's letters and some photos before they were thrown out by the bailiffs when Granny's farm was taken into the receivers to recover debts. Other relevant bits and photos came from my Father, Arthur, his eldest son.

Many thanks go to Kerstin Jeapes at Wycliffe Hall who understands photocopiers and associated technology for copying and emailing necessary texts and images. Also, to the Queen's Royal Hussars' newest subaltern at the time who was detailed to identify exchanges between Reginald Hoare and Winston Churchill in the QRH Officers' Mess suggestions book.

My thanks also go to Helion & Company proprietor Duncan Rogers for his interest when shown the letters and to Helion commissioning editor Dr Michael Lo Cicero for his interest, support and editorial efforts. We hope to publish Grandfather's Boer War journal and photos in due course. No thanks are complete without including my wife Liz who wrote her book while I was occupied with this tome.

Rev. Toddy Hoare
Holton
Oxfordshire
August 2018

Introduction

We do actually know when my grandfather, Reginald Hoare, popped the question to Violet Reid (the "Miss Walker recipient of the letters herein). We can only surmise that, having taken advantage of a lull in the on-going campaign in France, it was whilst on home leave to take in some grouse shooting. Letter 58 tells us it was 18 August 1918, a month before his 53rd birthday, so probably spent in a grouse butt. When my cousin retrieved the letters that RH had written to our future grandmother during 1915-18, it seemed a waste not to share the content for its social and military worth for future generations before such snippets are discarded by grandchildren oblivious of content. As a Regular Army cavalry officer, RH would have been in his element if the First World War had been more of what he experienced in South Africa during 1901-02, commanding a mobile column and screen of mounted scouts – his journal and photos is another volume filled with fascinating details of campaigning on the veldt. As the First World War was primarily fought dismounted, the common cavalry experience was trench warfare or scrambling up rocky wadis to the detriment of army issue boots. The desert was not all sand, it was an alien and hostile environment where horses could not operate except as beasts of burden and where the basic training as infantryman for every trooper came into play! The letters are essentially a courtship by correspondence which accounts for the title reflecting the addressee in the first exchange: "Dear Miss Walker". What was a cast becoming a twinkle in the eye of an old fisherman landing his catch! No replies exist as RH only kept the penultimate letter along with the latest as he needed to travel light. Grannies also tend to be hoarders of the romantic, so his correspondence, some of which was suspected to have gone to the bottom of the sea unseen, survives. However, there is also a wealth of excellent military information, especially if taken alongside the division and regimental histories that I have drawn on!

All forms of horsemanship were encouraged in the Victorian/Edwardian army. Indeed, a fund provided by Queen Victoria still subsidises hunting for Household Cavalry subalterns to improve their skills and confidence on horseback. RH was a renowned polo player as indeed was RH's 4th Queen's Own Hussars contemporary Winston Churchill when he could play.[1] Moreover, Violet's father was also a regular player and breeder of polo ponies from sought after stock. Indeed, one group of particularly fine specimens were

---

[1] Two exchanges in the 4th QOH officers' mess suggestion book provides insight into the rapport between 2nd Lt. Winston Spencer Churchill (WSC) and RH, in his capacity as regimental mess committee president, when dealing with the notoriously bumptious subaltern. WSC: "Why is the toast under the poached eggs always soggy?" RH: "Quite rightly. I have myself been within the kitchen and personally instructed the cook in the art of culinary. If the eggs are not eaten immediately they set up steam under the dish cover and the best and driest toast in the world becomes sodden. Would you like them done on croutes of fried bread?" WSC: "In the opinion of WSC the general comfort and furnishings of this mess being much below the standards of other cavalry regiment ... fresh furniture ... new wallpaper ... more suitable to the dignity of this regiment read WSC." RH: Having circled the WSC's points, observed: "Where? Price? Pattern? How? Shall be done. (Wallpaper). For dignity of regiment". Special thanks to Ben Fyfe who was, at the time of my mess book query, the newest subaltern in the QRH. See also, Winston Churchill, *My Early Life* (London: Eland, 2000).

Brigadier-General Reginald Hoare, c. 1918.

transported from Syria! Issue equipment changed with the coming of position warfare, but how we deployed our tanks or formed column and patrolled still reflected marking out a covert to catch a fox. Come 1914, Grandfather was an experienced cavalry officer of the traditional school knocking 50. He was ideal for leading Yeomanry who were still paid for taking their own horses to camp, because that was his world. As the worldwide conflict continued, the War Office appointed younger men to high command, so preferment was not to follow despite RH's visit to the War Office following Gallipoli, after which he was back to his old mounted brigade in Egypt. GOC 74th (Yeomanry) Division Major-General Eric Girdwood's letter is a great tribute to RH and the respect younger men[2] had for him! Although both operationally and tactically the order of battle proscribed that brigade HQ

---

2   See Appendix IV. While we can learn much about RH's character, temperament and generalship from his letters, there are two personal cameos where his troopers have their say. Both, as recorded in *The Yeomanry of Devon* and the *Proud Trooper*, stem from the early days of raising and training his mounted brigade, though the second anecdote was related first-hand by a member and old comrade when I took their service at Ayr in late 1980: A Devon Yeoman, on being asked who was the Brigadier, readily observed, "OI sim 'e be t'old gentleman with the red hat as goes abart with squire Bampfylde." Bampfylde was his brigade major at the time. Ayrshire Yeomanry. On inspection of a somewhat shambolic guard, RH, setting one of them on his horse to return in 10 minutes, he set to showing them how to do it properly by joining their ranks. Detailing who did what and how they retired to the guard room until the sound of horse approaching was overheard. "Right lads", RH exclaimed, "it's the bloody general. Turn out sharpish." The final tribute must be from his divisional commander, Major-General Eric Girdwood (GOC 74th Division) who admitted that he much appreciated advice from an older soldier who had no problems with being commanded by a younger man.

Reginald Hoare on Marengo, c. 1900.

should be behind regimental HQs, RH's correspondence with Violet demonstrate he often led from the front, thus it is interesting to look at his early military service record as a means of determining acquired military skills: Passing out of the Royal Military College in January 1886, he was duly commissioned into the 4th Queens Royal Hussars (QOH). Promoted captain in 1893, major in 1899 and lieutenant-colonel and CO of 4th QOH in 1905, it was during this period in RH's military career that he saw service in India (1900-01) and South Africa (1901-02). Following active service with 2nd Mounted Division during 1914-15, he was promoted brigade commander in March 1916.

It is interesting that RH attended Eton and WSC Harrow – I did Elementary and Intermediate Riding Courses with the Household Cavalry in Windsor in 1974, so like RH passed elementary veterinary and farriery! The choice of 4th QOH Hussars for RH suggests that either it was because the regiment was posted locally at the time or more likely that his mother was acquainted with the colonel, but it can be proven that in 1906 RH was responsible for adding the motto *Mente et Manu* to the regimental cap badge by Royal Warrant.[3] Of the First World War years, I will let the letters speak for themselves. RH described himself as a lame old gentleman, the result of a serious polo accident that caused him to rely on a stick for extra support to get around. As orders were shouted, there was much other shouting and "strafing" to reprimand or correct, but his men subsequently admitted, as he did himself, his bark was often worse than his bite. Of course, this was utilised as a means of getting the best out of everyone.

---

3   See Brig. Robin Rhoderick-Jones, *In Peace and War: The Story of The Queen's Royal Hussars (the Queen's Own and Royal Irish) Commissioned by Trustees of QRH* (Barnsley: Pen & Sword, 2018).

Following the war RH would have continued with his military career, but, despite friends in high places keeping a look out for training brigade employment, there were too many Brig- Generals laid off during peacetime reductions. 1919 saw the award of a CMG and family tradition has it that he was offered the post of Governor General of Gambia but, newly married, declined to take a young wife or raise children there. They retired to Badger near Wolverhampton and Shifnal. Violet's parents resided nearby at Ruckley Grange, Tong. A steward at Wolverhampton and Ludlow racecourses, RH's father-in-law was a member of the Jockey Club along with his brother Col. Willie Hall Walker who was a successful horse breeder better known as "Lord Wavertree". Whilst the Badger home was rented, a residence in Tomatin, Inverness was purchased and extended. This home was near popular Findhorn fishing sites and Violet's parents who had a shooting estate at Clun. As it was, the Second World War years were, Badger having been appropriated for the duration, spent in Scotland.

A family friend who subsequently joined RH's second son John in the Black Watch, recalls going shooting with RH round Balvraid and stocking the larder with welcome rabbits or any other game in season! Meantime, Violet was quite an entrepreneur establishing an extra fresh rations market garden at Clun and being one of the first to do battery hens as a novel means of supplying eggs to Inverness.! Quite a stir was caused at Tomatin Post Office after El Alamein when a telegram from the Prime Minister was sent to RH stating: "I have seen your son. He is fit and well." This was my Father, Arthur, by then a subaltern troop leader with the 4th Hussars which, three-fourths of the original draft had been captured in Greece in 1941, was in reserve during the battle. RH enjoyed his retirement years fishing in Scotland. He is actually buried at Dalarassie on the Findhorn near one of his favourite pools. RH died at Inverness on the operating table three weeks before I was born whilst a colostomy was in the process of being tidied up. My eldest sister remembers him as tall with log thin legs, rather fierce and of the mindset that small children should be seen and not heard. Thus she spent her time with the butler polishing the silver! In fact, he bestowed the nickname "Min" for her efforts in catching minnows for fishing bait. RH and Violet had four children:

Arthur b. 1920-2015: Eton, Faraday House; Sandhurst; electrical engineer; Major QOH 1941-53; ran D & M Training School, Cyprus 1942-44, RAC Demonstration Sqn. Warminster 1946; RSO Malaya 1948-50; Armour Development, Chobham 1950-52; East Africa, Mau-Mau 1953; established engineering firm Kenya to 1966; married Lucy Corbett-Winder (1915-90), daughter of Revd. E.H. Corbett-Winder and Myrtle (née Bardwell of East Yorkshire) West Stafford, Dorchester, Dorset 1940 ; divorced 1955.

John, 1925-49: Eton and Sandhurst; Capt. The Black Watch, MC 1944, killed in action Malaya 1949 whilst attached to the Cameron Highlanders following duty as jungle school instructor.

Robin, 1927-99: Eton and Sandhurst; Capt. 4th QOH; resigned commission; Adjutant Shropshire Yeomanry; farmed Hereford cattle in Gloucester.

Rosemary,1929: Married David Hodges who farmed near the pedigree Jersey dairy farm Violet established (1948-49) at Redmarley, Gloucester following RH's passing.

Toddy Hoare, Holton, Oxford, August 2018

Correspondence 1915–18
Gallipoli 1915

1.(20.6.15)

HdQuarters
Great Bentley Essex
June 20

Dear Miss Walker,

I managed to snatch a few hours leave from my military duties and motored over to Newmarket on Tuesday last, where I saw your father, & he very kindly asked me up to Cabrach to shoot in August.[1]

I should love to come and do so hope I shall be able to manage it. I have had no leave since war broke out and have not slept away from my Brigade for a single night, except upon one occasion when I was sent away on duty & had to spend a night at St Albans. So, I hope very much I shall be able to manage a few days leave in August if still in the country.

Will you ask your father what dates he wants me for I really think I shall be allowed to come as I have not been away at all from my work yet & shall look forward to my visit very much.

Are you ever in town now? You remember we met in the town once last year. I do run up for a few hours now and again when I have to go to the War Office. Do let me know if I can send you any Hurlingham or Ranelagh tickets. Kind regards to your Mother.

Sincerely yours
Reginald Hoare

⚜

2. (14.9.15)

Great Bentley
Essex

Dear Violet,

(I say, is that all right? or is it beastly cheek & horridly familiar? ought I to say, "Dear Miss Walker"?)

Thanks for your charming and interesting letter. I have also sent you up some "ante-midge" stuff which I am told is good, some "Larola" which you will find v. nice to use & especially useful in the winter before going out into a cold 'N. Easter', and the last thing I have sent off was a parcel, addressed to your mother, containing two bottles of the best Marmalade I know, & I hope you will enjoy it.

---

1   Cabrac ("Antler Place") is located in Moray/Aberdeen just off the A941 south of Dufftown and Bridgend and West of Elrick. About 1916-17, Violet's father purchased Clun at Tomatin from the Macintosh family of Moy who were struggling with a grand design there because of wartime shortages of building material.

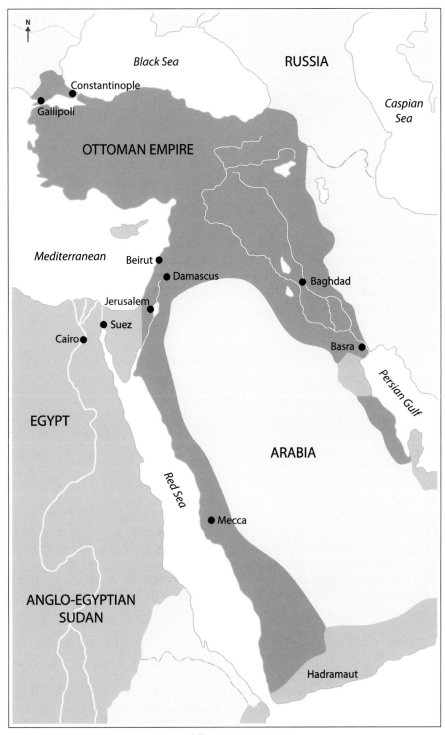

Middle East 1914-18.

I was much interested to hear of the good day on Tormichelt: how I wish I had been with you in a butt in the same place, but I am glad to hear ...

Col: Rutherford got 40 of them "under the chin".

We expect to get off somewhere about the 20th, but certainly not before that date.

Do write me a line out there sometimes & tell me your news. I feel a very 'lonely soldier' sometimes and am glad of letters from friends.

I <u>did</u> enjoy my visit to you this year. I had been nowhere else for a visit for a year. I wonder if we shall be in Constantinople by Xmas. I hope and expect we shall be there before that.

The accounts of the Zepp [lin] raid are quite amusing. People were walking about London, and on their roofs in all sorts of attire – Gentlemen in the streets in pyjamas (*sic*) & overcoat: Ladies in Nighties & cloaks & everybody excited & watching the Zepp which could be clearly seen lit up by our searchlights, & you could see the incendiary bombs being dropped, & also the British shells from ante-aircraft guns bursting near it.

One German bomb wiped out a motor bus with people in it completely, or the casualties would have been fewer, & we had our first man wounded in the Brigade. He was a Yeoman at Liverpool St Station whose finger was cut by falling glass.

No more now.

Kind regards to you all,

Yrs. v. sincerely

Reginald Hoare

≈◦ ◦≈

3. (3.11.15)

2nd S. Western Mounted Bde
Mediterranean Exp: Force
Nov. 3rd

Dear Violet,

Many thanks for your letter of Oct: 7th, and I am interested to learn that the last effort of the village photographer at Great Bentley is approved of. Thanks too for the little snapshot of yourself, which is very good I think – you certainly look very "merry & bright" in it.

Yes, you must all be very anxious about Gwynne, and I trust you will have heard ere this of his safety after the splendid advance made about Loos.

We had a good voyage out here, but it was not without its thrills of excitement, as they tried to torpedo us, but 'a miss is as good as a mile' and now here we are living in "dug outs" on the Northern shore of the Gallipoli peninsular, overlooking the entrance to the Gulf of Saros.

We get a daily shelling by the Turks, and I am sorry to say he has already caused some casualties in my Brigade. We shell him back again with guns ashore and afloat, and we hope we do them more damage than they does us. They are reported short of ammunition for their guns, but they celebrate occasional festivals or birthdays, or the arrival of a fresh consignment of ammunition, by giving us an extra dose of shrapnel; but they do wonderfully little damage on the whole, and the men take very little notice of the "bricks" being thrown at them – in fact they are rather inclined to take too much of an interest in watching the

Highland Barricade, Suvla Bay. (Ogilvie, *The Fife and Forfar Yeomanry and 14th (F. & F. Yeo.) Battn. R.H. 1914-1919*)

effect of the last shell, and so run the chance of being "biffed" by the next once that comes.

A few deserters from the Turkish army come in nearly every day, & we also had a few by nightwork in the trenches.

I go into the trenches nearly every day for a few hours and go up there tomorrow for a week; but really one is safer in the trenches than walking about 2 miles in rear of them, as you never know where you may get in the way of a chance shell. Those Turks are so careless.

I hope you finished the grouse shooting well, and the family are very flourishing.

With kind regards

Yours v. sincerely

Reginald Hoare

4. (5.12.15)

2nd S. Western Mounted Bde
"Galley Poley" Peninsular
Dec 5

Dear Violet,

Here's to wish you all the best of good wishes for Xmas and 1916, and I hope that long before another Christmas has come the war will be over.

We had a very rough time of it in the trenches lately, as we first got a tremendously heavy storm with deluges of rain, which turned the trenches into rivers, and they emptied themselves into our "dug-outs". We were literally washed out of them, & the water rose so suddenly that some officers lost everything. I luckily was able to save my valise & bedding, but now brush my hair with a nail brush – my proper hairbrush with numerous other articles having been washed away in the flood.

After the rain had stopped the wind suddenly shifted round from S.W to N.E, and for 36 hours we had a terrific blizzard with snow and hard frost.

The conditions for the men in the trenches were most trying, as most of them were wet through to the skin. Several were frost-bitten as the cold was intense, & there was nearly an inch of ice on the water in the trenches, and the water was over one's knees. Several men were frostbitten, and it was a very storm-battered crowd which hobbled back when we were relieved.

It was far worse for the Turks than for us, as they are for the most part poorly clad, and we hear that many died of exposure.

Now the weather has turned warmer, & we are slowly thawing and getting dry again. We were told to expect bad weather in January but this storm coming at the end of November found us quite unprepared.

I hope the family is all well and that you have good news of Gwynne, I suppose you are working hard with the V. A. D, but I hope you have been able to get a day or two hunting & have enjoyed good sport.

How very near your father was to winning the Cesarewitch. I wish he could have won it. I hope you all had your bit on "for a place".

We got a shower of shells from the Turk about mid-day today, and I had two within 20 yards of me, and some shrapnel bullets through my mackintosh. N.B. I was not in the mackintosh.

Well, when the Turk shells us we give him back two for one, & I hope our shells do him more harm than his do us.

Again, with kindest regards to you all, & every good wish for Xmas & 1916.

Yrs v. sincerely

Reginald Hoare

Egypt and Palestine 1916-18

5. (14.2.16)

Alexandria
Feb 14th

Dear Violet,

Many thanks for your letter of Jan 27th which reached me yesterday.

It was very kind of you to write me a letter for Xmas but I am sorry to say it has never reached me. Never mind. Write me another.

Please thank your father for his letter written from Nice. I am so glad to hear that Gwynne is quite fit again and has been enjoying himself at home. You will have heard all about how we outwitted and completely hoodwinked the Turks and got away from the

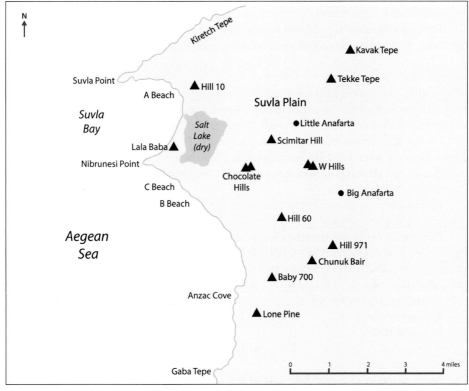

N

Kiretch Tepe

Kavak Tepe

Suvla Point

Tekke Tepe

Hill 10

A Beach

Suvla Plain

Suvla
Bay

Salt
Lake
(dry)

Little Anafarta

Scimitar Hill

Lala Baba

Nibrunesi Point

W Hills

Chocolate
Hills

C Beach

Big Anafarta

B Beach

Hill 60

Aegean
Sea

Hill 971

Chunuk Bair

Baby 700

Anzac Cove

Lone Pine

Gaba Tepe

0   1   2   3   4 miles

Suvla Bay, 1915.

Peninsular without their ever knowing that we were going, till we were gone.

We have been here now over a month, though we expected to be moved to Cairo or some other part of Egypt a few days after we landed; but here we are still, and much enjoying this glorious winter climate and sunshine.

No hunting here, but I have been out duck shooting and snipe shooting a few times. My best day after duck was 46 duck and teal to my own gun, or rather to the Belgian gun which I borrowed for the day. And 22 couple of snipe was our best day – very tiring walking through the black mud of the Nile delta.

This afternoon I have been playing some lawn tennis on the excellent hard courts at the "Sporting Club", where there is a small racecourse, golf links, polo ground and a lot of tennis courts.

I expect we shall remain in Egypt for another month or two, and then be moved to France or wherever we are most wanted. I think the authorities have come to the conclusion that this is a very good centre for troops to spend the winter in, especially as it possesses a far better climate than England, & it is quite easy to get to France, Salonika, Mesopotamia, or East Africa from here.

Lady Tullibardin & Lady Howard de Walden both have hospitals for convalescents here, and (old) Lady Carnarvon and her sister are also here, doing a lot of good work among the soldiers.

We have a large cinema tent in Camp, and a Y. M. C. A. hut, so there is everything here to make the men comfortable, and there are any number of donkeys for the men to ride.

I got up a Donkey Gymkhana for my men – hired 40 donkeys for the afternoon, & had a tug of war on donkeys, and a race with the riders sitting facing the donkeys' tails. You never heard such laughter. The men thoroughly enjoyed it. The relaxation was a real treat to them after the hard time & discomforts of the Gallipoli Peninsular. I did not allow any whips, sticks, or spurs to be used in any of the donkey races, and the race for donkey boys (40) on their feet without their donkeys, was most picturesque. Most of them held their skirts of their long smocks in their teeth as they ran.

I am so glad to hear the new horse is a success, & that you have enjoyed some good hunts. I wonder when I shall be hunting again. I have <u>hopes</u> that the war will be over before next Xmas. The air is full of rumours, one is that the Kaiser is really seriously ill, and has 3 double to impersonate him.

I hear I am to be given a bigger command, but the business is not quite fixed up yet, so perhaps it will come to nothing after all – Wait & see.

Please tell your father that the case of lager beer he kindly offered to send me, did not turn up, so I expect he had time to stop it when he heard of the evacuation. Here we can get everything, and live in comparative luxury in tents, which are much better than damp, cold, dugouts.

Kindest regards to you all
V. sincerely yours
Reginald Hoare

My correct address is:
2nd S. Western Mounted Bde Base M.E.F., Egypt.

⁓☙ ❧⁓

6. (6.4.16)

Shepheard's Hotel Cairo
April 6th

Dear Violet,
Please tell your father not to think of sending out any more of the splendid lager beer to me, as when you get this I shall be on my way home.

Lord Kitchener wants a rest, so I am coming home to take his place for a bit. (I <u>don't</u> think). Seriously I <u>don't</u> quite know what is in store for me at home but expect to be sent out to France soon with some command, as I have lately had two increased commands in this country.

I hope if you come to London you will let me know, so that we can drive away all thoughts of the War and the new Budget at a play & have a good laugh.

I hope you are very fit and well and all beginning to get your "summer coats" and pulling double.

Kindest regards to you all.
Yours v. sincerely
Reginald Hoare

Naval & Military Club
94 Piccadilly, will always find me.

❧

7. (30.4.16)
Telegrams & Station, Culkerton.

Trull
Tetbury
Gloucestershire April 30th

Dear Violet,
Here I am home again, and I have to thank you for a charming long letter, which followed me home, telling me all about your foxhunting, coot hunting, moor-hen hunting & other sports.

It is very nice to be home again, but what a week of bad news it has been with the loss of a battleship, the fall of Kut, the Irish Rebellion with loss of life, and the Yeomanry in a mess in Egypt. I am glad to say these latter were not in my Brigade.

I have not heard yet what my next job is going to be, and, in the mean time I am enjoying a very pleasant rest.

Do let me know if you are likely to come to London so that we could meet & do a play.

I should so much like to have the chance of seeing you all, and of returning some of the hospitality which I have so enjoyed at Cabrach.

I may go down to Newmarket next week, & if I do I shall hope to meet your father, & perhaps you – but I don't think you are taken racing.

Kindest regards to you all,
Very sincerely yours
Reginald Hoare

The Naval & Military Club always finds me.

❧

8. (4.5.16)

Naval & Military Club
94, Piccadilly W.
Tel.No. Mayfair 6300
May 4th

Dear Violet,
Many thanks for your kind letter of welcome home. It was good of you to write it.

So sorry to hear about the horrid German measles and "flue". What a bore for you all, but I am glad to learn you are now practically all right. Take care of yourself & don't go & get a nasty chill on the top of it all.

I went to Newmarket yesterday, and met your father looking v. fit & well. He kindly asked me to Ruckley this week end, but I refused as I did not think you would be back –

will you? However, I shall see him there again tomorrow, when perhaps he will know more about your movements; I would not like to go there & miss seeing you.

Please thank your mother too for kindly asking me. I have never been to Ruckley and shall look forward very much to seeing you there.

I found it very cold at Newmarket yesterday & I lost my money but was cheered by meeting many friends.

Kindest regards to you all
Yours v. sincerely
Reginald Hoare

---

9. (6.5.16)

Naval & Military Club
94, Piccadilly.
W. Tel. No. Mayfair 6300
May 6th

Dear Violet,
Many thanks for your postcard & the kind invitation it contained.

I have spent half the day at the War Office & tried hard to get away but could not manage it. I have been given command of a Brigade in Kent & am told to start work there at once but have wired to my Divisional Commander for 10 days leave before taking up the appointment. I am awaiting his answer, so that I can reply to your postcard. I might be able to come by the 6 pm if the answer comes in time. The only Sunday train is a flier & takes 5 hours, but it can't be helped.

Sorry not to be able to send a reply earlier.

Kindest regards to you all, & I hope all invalids are quite recovered and are "pulling double".

Yrs v. sincerely
Reginald Hoare

---

10. (18.5.16)

Headquarters
10th Mounted Brigade
Wrotham
Kent
May 18th

Dear Violet,
I am sorry I shall miss you. I am writing this in my tent before breakfast having just received your letter.

I have been down here since Monday, and and up to my eyes in work, as a "new broom" I find plenty to do, and in addition to my commanding this Brigade, I am temporarily in command of the whole Division which necessitates my dividing my time between here & Tilbury, so I am kept pretty well on the move.

This place is on the main London-Dover road. Its a very pretty country, but very hilly, and the yeomanry who are now on bicycles very much wish it was flatter!

Do let me know beforehand when you are next coming to London. I wish you were staying over Sunday.

Kindest regards
Yrs v. sincerely
Reginald Hoare

Hasn't the Bondamere bracelet turned up yet?

≈≈≈

11. (31.5.16)

Headquarters
10th Mounted Brigade
Wrotham
Kent
May 31st

Dear Violet,
Many thanks for your letter of 25th.

Yes, it was very unfortunate that you should have come up to town just as I had been ordered to take up my appointment and was up to my eyes in work.

Will you try and let me know beforehand another time, so that I can make arrangements to be away for a day – that is if you would really, really like to see me again.

The Divisional General has returned, but I cannot take a day's leave without letting him know beforehand, so it all takes a little thinking out and organising. I hope you found some nice hats & frocks to suit your taste, and that they won't disguise you too much, so that I shan't know you again.

Talking of hats & frocks, I wish you'd send me one of your latest photos that you were talking to me about, though I know you did not like them; but perhaps I shall.

I took a day off yesterday and went to Newmarket for this "New Derby" but came back a poorer & sadder man as I backed the 2nd.

I saw your father there looking very fit. I had to return the same night in case of Zepp raids.

I hope you enjoyed the Chelsea Flower Show & met lots of friends. I trust Monica is quite fit again now.

Glad to hear they have repaired the bracelet to your liking.

Yours v. sincerely
Reginald Hoare

≈≈≈

12. (10.6.16)

Headquarters
10th Mounted Brigade
Wrotham
June 10th

Dear Violet,

Many thanks for your letter and the photos. The big one of you on your hunter is a photo of a very smart young lady in hunting dress – but as I have never seen you in that attire, it does not remind me of you as I should wish it to do. I hope you don't mind my saying so. You sent a small one of it to me many months ago, and I have it still.

Next time anybody is busy with a Kodak, do get them to take a photo of you in your ordinary dress and garden hat – as I know you best; and don't let them stand miles away so that you come out too tiny. It is not necessary to take it full length. You can get quite good half-length photos with a Kodak by standing much closer. Let's have one your hat on & one with hat off.

I hope to be able to get up to town when you next come, but it's no certainty. I am in command of the whole division again this weekend & have got to stay here – <u>Drat</u> this war.

On Monday I am to practice my Brigade crossing the Thames from Gravesend to Tilbury in ferry steamers, and it will be a time test, with Lord French looking on.

The packing away of men and bicycles on a steamer requires some thinking out and organisation. I hope to goodness we get a fine day for it.

I should think the grey evening frock will be very becoming & I shall look forward to seeing you in it but I fear that a few hours in the afternoon is all I shall be able to get leave for. Never mind – We must "wait & see".

Post just going.
Yours very sincerely
Reginald Hoare

13. (18.6.16)

Headquarters
10th Mounted Brigade
Wrotham
June 18th

Dear Violet,

I am off again. I yesterday read a wire telling me to hold myself in readiness to proceed to Egypt on receipt of passage instructions, having been appointed to the command of the 2nd Dismounted Bde out there.

The "passage instructions" have not yet reached me, so I don't expect I shall be "pushed off" this week. Friday is the usual P&G day for sailing, & I expect I shall go by P&O, as there are not so many transports running out to the East now as there were when we were in the Dardanelles.

Drat this war. I wish I wasn't going out there again at this time of year. It is <u>very</u> hot out there now. 112 in the shade. Its icy cold here in camp, & I am writing this with a thick rug over my knees.

My successor here will be General Williams, and I hand over command to him on Wednesday, and shall be in London Naval & Mil: Club after that till I sail. I will let you know as soon as I know when that will be.

My address in Egypt will be
2nd Dismounted Bde
E. E. F. Egypt
No grouse shooting for me this year, I don't think.
Drat this war.
Kindest regards to you all.
Yrs very sincerely
Reginald Hoare

꧁ ꧂

14. (24.6.16)

Naval and Military Club 94, Piccadilly W
Tel.No. Mayfair 6300
June 24th

Dear Violet,
Many thanks for your kind letter & wire. The letter arrived at Wrotham after I had left, and when I got it I was so rushed that I missed the point that you might be expecting me this weekend.

The wire I have only just (6pm) received, as I left London early this morning, to run down into the country to say 'Goodbye' to a sister. I am sorry to appear so remiss in not answering before.

I embark at Devonport tomorrow, and my address in Egypt will be:
2nd Dismounted Brigade
E.E.F.
Egypt
So that's the place to send the snap shots to.

It is very unsettling to be sent back to Egypt in this unexpected way, but war is unsettling, isnt it? I was just beginning to get settled down to my Brigade at home, & liked it, when they whisk me off again. Well, a soldier has got to do what he is told and go where he is sent.

If you should meet a Major Lascelles up at the camp, please remember me to him. He was my Brigade Major at the beginning of the War.

I hope the grouse won't turn out quite so bad as the report. I have had to refuse another Scotch invitation.

Kindest regards to all at Ruckley & I hope your father will win some good races this summer.

Now I must go and finish my packing, as I leave London tomorrow morning.

There was a rumour in the club last night that we had made a good advance near Lille & taken a lot of prisoners, but there's nothing about it in the papers today, so I suppose rumour lied. I was also told that the good "push" lately done by the Russians, is <u>nothing</u> to the big push they are going to do later on further North. I hope it will be true.

Au revoir.

Best of luck to you.

Yours v. sincerely

Reginald Hoare

I got both your letters & shall look forward to getting others in Egypt.

15.(4.7.16)

S.S.*Northland*
In the Mediterranean
July 4th

Dear Violet,

We have been very lucky with the weather and have had nothing but smooth water since we sailed. There was certainly a very slight swell for the first two days, which proved too much for some of the men, but they must have been very bad sailors. Since then it has been wonderfully smooth, and the Bay of Biscay was on its best behaviour.

We just touched at Gib and are now nearing Malta where this will be posted.

This is a very comfy & steady ship, and as I am in command of all the troops on board, I have got a <u>very</u> good 4-berth cabin to myself, and if it were not for the war and other reasons the voyage would be most enjoyable. But we have to put up with a lot of discomfort due to the war, as we sail without lights at night, and so can only sit about in the dark on deck after dinner – all ports are kept closed in case of a torpedo, so the heat in the cabins is very unpleasant. The smoking room is the only room lit up after dinner, but with every port closed the atmosphere in it becomes too thick for me, and I prefer the deck in the dark, to the thick smoke & "froust" of the lighted smoking room.

We have no chaplain on board, but I had a church parade on Sunday and did the service myself & had to lead off the hymns as we had no music. I think the men liked the service, and it breaks up the monotony of a long day at sea.

I had very bad news just as we were sailing as I heard of the death of one of my sisters from pleurisy & pneumonia.[2] She was only ill a few days having caught a bad chill. I went down to the country to say "Goodbye" to her and am very glad now that I did so. All this made my departure from home a very sad one, so you must write me some nice letters to cheer me up when you have time.

I wonder if your trip to London has come off, & whether you enjoyed it. I hope so.

We get the wireless news every morning, and it is all very cheering, and I hope the advance will continue to be successful.

I have been reading one of Ian Hay's books "Happy go lucky". Such a charming book. Have you read it? I am sure you will like it. (1/- at a bookstall.) We have got a large sail bath rigged on deck for the men, and they are in and out of it all day long like a lot of ducks. There is always fresh sea water running through it, so it is kept very clean & refreshing.

---

2   Bee, the third youngest of RH's sisters. See Appendix I. Assisted by the youngest of 14 siblings Ivy. See letter 63.

I am writing this on the bridge of which I am made an honorary member as O.C. troops, and I get a nice breeze up here, and am glad of it, as it beginning to get fairly hot now (80) but nothing to what I shall find it when I get to Egypt where it is now about 110 in the shade.

I only found one officer on board whom I knew, but he was an old friend of mine, & we were very pleased to meet each other again.

I hope Monica is quite fit and well now, and that you are all going strong.

I wonder when I shall have another ride with you & a lark over fences. I <u>did</u> so enjoy that ride.

I hope the rock garden is very flourishing, and the race horses are giving promise of becoming regular "gold mines".

I liked the little photo of you cut out of a group and shall look forward to getting the other snap shots of you.

Kindest remembrances to the family, and all good wishes.

Yours very sincerely

Reginald Hoare

— ✢ ✢ —

16. (29.7.16)

2nd Dismounted Me E. E. F.
July 29

Dear Violet,

Many thanks for your kind and sympathetic letter. I too have to offer my condolence on the sad loss you have all sustained on the death of your cousin.[3]

This a wild, hot spot on the edge of the Western desert on the way out to the Kharga Oasis.

Since I arrived out here I have been given an increased command and am now responsible for about 300 miles of the Western frontier from Assonan (Aswan) northwards, so I have plenty to do, as I have to command my Brigade as well. I am shortly starting out on a tour round my "dominions", to inspect the various detachments of my mighty army.

Its beastly blisteringly hot here and we live in shorts & shirtsleeves. The temperature is frequently up to 110 in the shade and is generally still over 100 as late as 5 pm. The nights only begin to get cool just as its time to get up again (5 AM). If you like it <u>really</u> hot you would enjoy this. But it's too hot to be pleasant. Electric fans don't exist, and for some reason Indian Punkahs are unknown. Egypt is sadly behind the times (drat the pen) in many up-to-date dodges which make for comfort.

You just love it when it is really hot, do you. Well, have you ever tried 110 in the shade? That means that everything is 110. Your cold bath is 110. The towel you dry yourself is 110; your "undies" are 110, your "nighty" would be 110, & the pillow & sheets would be 110. When it is over 100, I think you'd find it too hot to be pleasant. One takes <u>such</u> a long time getting cool. Our ice bill is very big, & we are lucky to be able to get it at all. The ice has to

---

3   Captain George Trevor Cartland: Winchester and Sandhurst 1911; Adjutant 1st Rifle Brigade; KIA France 1 July 1916. There is a photo of him in uniform to which RARH, eldest son of RH, bears a remarkable resemblance!

come all the way from Cairo, & the blocks are sadly reduced in size by the time they arrive. I quite envy your paddling in a nice cool brook fishing for big stones. I should love to have been with you.

I should like to see your garden now. <u>Wh</u>at a change it would be from this bare, baking hot desert, which is treeless.

So glad you liked Newmarket and I wish Blackadder had won instead of Nassovian.

So glad you like Ian Hays books. If you like to send me "the Safety Match" "Pip" & "a Man's Man", I should be very grateful, as we do no out of door work between 10 am and 5 pm; but I do a good deal of Office work then, & am writing this in my office, which is a poor sort of mud house – v. hot – but there is no fear of frostbite or chilblains – and after all one can't have everything.

Next month when "High Nile" comes, we may get some good sport rat-shooting, as the rats get flooded out of the cultivated land & come onto the dry desert.

Please don't apologise for the length of your "rambling" letter. I found it most interesting and I hope you will write me many more like it.

This should catch you at Cabrach, & I hope you will have nice weather while you are up there, & that you will not find the sport so bad, as the fish reports led you to suppose.

Kindest remembrances to you all.

Yours very sincerely

Reginald Hoare

~≈⊙≈~

17. (9.8.16)

2nd Dismounted Bde
E. E. F.
Aug 9th

Dear Violet,

Your pencil note written from the Cottage Hospital has just reached me.

I am <u>so</u> sorry to hear you have been laid up & had to have your tonsils out. Poor you. I <u>am</u> sorry. It must have been a horrid operation, and I fear you must have suffered a lot of pain & discomfort for many days afterwards.

I trust this will find you at Cabrach – convalescent, and comfortable and confident of having obtained a lasting benefit from the operation. I am only just back from an 8 days tour of inspection of my force, & travelled daily several miles by Railway, Motor & on horses.

It was all very interesting, but too hot to make it really enjoyable. The heat & dust in a railway carriage out here at this time of the year is pretty bad.

I went as far South as the Assonan (Aswan) Dam, which is a wonderful piece of engineering work, and saw the whole of the temple of Philce which will shortly be submerged when the Nile reaches its highest level. At present the Nile is a river of liquid chocolate to look at, and a beautifully refreshing (!) bath which I had in a private Bungalow near the Dam, had a fine collection of Nile mud at the bottom of it when I let the water run-off.

I found it very hot down there, temp: 112–116 – so that 100–105 of this place now seems quite moderate.

I generally slept in the saloon carriage placed at my disposal and I had it shunted & left in sidings when I wanted to sleep; but it was a most anti-deluvian old carriage, which made a deafening noise when it went along, and the first night we had to eat our dinner by the light of a borrowed Railway lantern, as we could not get the carriage lamps (gas) to light. To add to our discomfort, the natives presumably mistook my palatial (!) saloon for a 3rd Class carriage & would persist in boarding it with their dirty bags & baggage. I am afraid I handled some of them rather roughly.

You will by this time have read of the fight near the Suez Canal, but that is a far cry from here. My show is on the Western frontier, but I have a nephew there in command of a Horse Artillery Battery, and I am expecting to hear from him soon about it.

All my sympathies to you for the suffering you have been through, and I hope you will be all the better for your operation for the rest of your life.

Kindest regards to all at Cabrach, and I hope your father's cartridges are nice and straight this year.

Yours very sincerely
Reginald Hoare

18.(20.8.16)

Egypt
Aug 20th

Dear Violet,
I do so hope that by the time this reaches you, you are fit & well again and enjoying life with shooting parties at Cabrach.

I am just back from spending 4 days in the Kharga Oasis which is 90 miles across the desert & West of here.

We went there by the small narrow guage railway, and the train instead of taking 7 hours took 17½ hours. The engine broke down in the middle of the desert at about 4 pm when we were half way, and it was 11 pm before the relief train reached us. Luckily, we had some biscuits & drinks with us, & we just had to sit in the carriage nodding with sleep till we reached our destination. As it was supposed to be a daylight service, there were no lights in the carriage, so we could not read. But we could and did swear.

I was disappointed with the Oasis. I expected to find a sort of Garden of Eden, but with the exception of a few date palms & other trees, and small patches of cultivation near the Wells the Oasis was sandy & flat and uninviting.

The temperature there was 104–108 daily, but I cooled myself occasionally in a delightful swimming bath, the water for which came straight from a spring, and was at a temperature of 82, so it was pleasantly tepid.

So glad to see "Blackadder "won a race, & I hope your father will win many more before the year is out.

All good wishes for a speedy recovery & kindest remembrances to all at Cabrach.

Yrs v. sincerely
Reginald Hoare

19. (24.8.16)

Headquarters
2nd Dismounted Bde EEF
Egypt
24.8.16

Dear Violet,

I have lately returned from a trip to the Kharga Oasis, which is 105 miles West of here, and you get at the place by the little 2ft 6 inches railway across the intervening desert.

My journey there was not very enjoyable. The journey is supposed to take 7 hours, by my train it took 17½ hours, as we broke down in the middle of the desert, and had to wait there 10 hours till a.relief train came along and helped us in to our destination. Instead of arriving at 4 p.m., we did not arrive till 2.30 a.m. next morning. – It was most enjoyable – I don't think!

The railway commences with an ascent of about 1200 feet out of the Nile Valley, and this takes up 25–50 miles of the journey; then for 60–70 miles you go through a high-level desert, the scenery of which is constantly changing. – There are big expanses quite open and smooth – some covered with small stones like shingle; others appear to be almost paved, as they are covered with singularly regular shaped flat stones like paving stones. Again, you come across another flat expanse which is dotted with very round brown stones about the size of footballs, or large cannon balls, and it looks as if someone bad put then out in rows, 20 to 50 yards apart. Other portions of the desert are very rocky, the rocks assuming all shapes and sizes, and are white, grey or brown. – As you get nearer the Oasis you come upon large hillocks of "blown sand". These are constantly moving. The prevailing wind blows the sand from one side over the top, and it slowly trickles down the other side, and accumulates at the bottom like this:

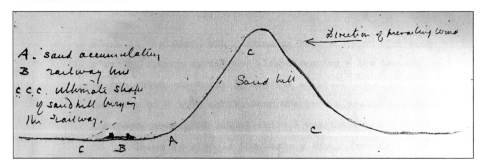

[A]s the train passed close to some sandhills, we could actually see the streams of sand steadily trickling down from the top to the bottom.

Where the sandhills are close to the railway and on the windward side of it, labourers have to be kept constantly at work shoveling the sand away, or the railway would get buried. During a heavy sandstorm this actually has happened, and the train was brought to a standstill and all hands had to get out and help clear the line. Upon this occasion I believe the journey took 25 hours, so my 17½ hours trip is not a record.

As the journey was supposed to be a daylight one there were no lamps in the train, so we could not read but sat nodding with sleep in our seats.

After passing the sandhills the railway decends again the 1200 feet into the basin of the Oasis.

I expected to find the Oasis a sort of Garden of Eden, with all sorts of luxuriant growth, but except for patches of cultivation round the wells and springs, and some groups of date palms, and a few other trees the rest is sandy desert – I was much disappointed with it.

The Oasis basin is about 60 miles long by 10–15 miles broad, and except for certain openings and passes through the hill is surrounded by the high escarpment of cliffs 1200 feet high. In most of the wells the water is warm, and the best thing I found in the Oasis was a swimming bath supplied with water straight from a spring and always running. The temperature of the water was about 82 degrees, so it did not give one anything of a cold shock, when one took a header into it.

I enjoyed some good bathes while I was there.

There is also at the Oasis a Roman Fort in a good state of preservation and an ancient temple or two, one of which was said to be one of Pierpoint Morgan's hunting grounds for relics.

I took a motor trip one day in a Ford car about 20 miles out into the desert further West, and found it just the same as any other desert; that is to say, miles and miles and miles and miles of nothing but desert, never a tree – but the surface of it was dotted with large and small hills and hillocks, and was more sandy than the desert round here., which is smoother and more gravelly. The car averaged about 12 miles an hour, and the number of times when we had to get out and shove behind to get through patches of extra soft sand was not many.

It was pretty hot in the Oasis – temperature 104–108 degrees daily; it has been a few degrees cooler here lately, the thermometer only just touching 100.

My journey back was without incident, only taking 8 or 9 hours – we are not particular to an 'hour or two!!

The Nile is now in flood and thousands of acres of land which were growing crops a month ago, have been cleared of their crops, and now are under water, and being fertilised by the deposit of rich Nile mud which will be left when the floods begin to go down. Several of the camps in the Section under my command have had to be moved in consequence, and it is quite difficult to find suitable camping ground, as the Nile Valley is so flat; and when you take a bath in the Nile Valley during "High Nile" the water is generally chocolate in colour, with a fine deposit of mud at the bottom of it.

Here we are just on the desert, and get our water from wells, and it is beautifully clean and good.

Rats flooded out by the rising Nile are beginning to be numerous in all the banks not under water.

The "High Nile" is a regular annual occurrence and looked forward to by the "fellahean" or petty farmer with keen interest. This year it promises to be a better flood than usual, which means that more acres will be fertilised and cultivated.

The poor old Turk got a nasty knock in this endeavour to attack the Suez Canal, and I should think it will be some time before he ventures on another attempt, tho' he may talk of doing so.

As the weather has got a few degrees cooler lately, the men have started playing football in the cool(?) of the evening, during the last 40 minutes of daylight. The football ground is heavy stoney sand, so I leave you to guess what the effort must be to run and kick a football about in that sort of going with the temperature at 90 degrees or more.

However, it says a lot for the men that they are so energetic. I am trying to get up rounders for the non-football players, and we are also hoping to get a cricket pitch of baked mud put out on the sand and covered with matting.

In spite of the heat the men have kept wonderfully well; but this is a desolate spot. We have occasional open-air concerts, one Regiment has got up a Glee club, and they also have a first-rate mouth-organ quartet. The concert generally includes some pipe playing, reels, and a sword dance by the Scotch Regiment.

I have got Lovat Scouts under me, and two Gows – sons of the Stalker at Killichonah are in this Rgt.

"Some" letter this, isn't it? It is almost the same as I wrote you last week, but I am sending copies of it round to my family, so had it type written to save one a lot of letter writing in the heat. You will see that its so hot, even the ink is running.

I do hope you are quite fit again & enjoying good sport & fine weather among the heather & grouse. I shall be interested to hear what sort of sport you get.

So glad to see "BlackAdder" won again beating Silver Tag. Hearty congratulation to your father, & more power to the stable.

Kindest regards to you all.

Yrs v. sincerely

Reginald Hoare

---

20. (11.9.16)

2nd Dismounted Bde E. E. F.
Sept 11th

Dear Violet,

Many thanks for your splendid long letter from Glenartney & the picture of the house. How pleased your mother must be to have such a charming garden, and it looks a delightful place.

I am so glad you are feeling so much better, but I expect you still have to be careful and guard against chills.

I hope Monica has got rid of the "pains under her pinny" all right, without any appendicitis. I expect it gave her a bit of a fright.

You do not tell me who your guns have been, and now are. But there. I always want to know too much. I am glad to say the temperature has cooled off a bit, and the men are playing football in the sandy, dusty, gravelly desert every evening – temp about 86 to 90, so one can still look on without wanting an overcoat.

The only excitement we have had lately has been two accidents in one week on the little desert railway which runs out from here to the Oasis 100 miles away.

These Native Engine drivers are no good, & can neither drive up hill, nor down, and they let the train run away with them going downhill into the Oasis, and 5 natives were killed in the first accident, & 1 British soldier & 4 natives killed in the second accident which occurred near the same place. We had 11 trucks and one engine smashed up, and they are very hard to replace out here.

Thanks 1,000 times for sending the books: they have not come yet but will arrive this week I expect.

Kindest regards to you all.

Yrs very sincerely

Reginald Hoare

⁂

21. (30.9.16)

2nd Dismounted Bde E. E. F.

Sept 30th

Dear Violet,

Many thanks for your splendid long letter from Glenartney, and for the charming little photo case & photos. I think the one I have kept is excellent, but, please, these two are not in focus, so I return them. What a trial I am. Try again.

I had another trip to the Kharga Oasis last week, doing the 100 miles along the Desert railway in a railway motor trolly. But we broke down badly on our way back; one of the wheels collapsed, and there we were in the middle of the desert.

Luckily, we were only 2½ miles from a ganger's hut with a telephone to it, so we telephoned for another motor trolly to come out to us, & it reached us about mid-night, & we got hone at 3. AM. It was very lucky we spotted the wheel giving way, & before it finally collapsed, or we should have had a bad accident. *As* it was the final collapse came while we were pushing the old trolly 2 miles to the nearest siding near the ganger's hut, & we did have a job to get it the last mile after the final collapse.

What a ripping place Glenartney must be from your description, and what topping sport you had. Well done Monica getting her stag. I hope she got a Royal before she came down.

His Imperial Majesty the Czar of Russia, has, with the approval of His Majesty the King, bestowed upon me (and two other officers out here) "the Order of St Stanislaus (2nd Class with Sword) in recognition of Distinguished Service during the Campaign".

I am afraid I cannot plead guilty to any Distinguished Service during the Campaign, but I shall be very pleased to make the acquaintance of "old man Stanislaus". I hope he will do me a lot of good. I am told it is a very good order to get.

Many thanks for sending the books. I expect they will arrive by next mail. Parcels are generally a week or more behind letters.

It's a good deal cooler out here now but I still sleep out on the verandah, with only one very thin blanket over me.

So glad you are so fit again, & I hope the throat has by this time ceased from troubling you altogether.

Kindest regards to all at Ruckley.

Yrs v. sincerely

Reginald Hoare

The Kharga Oasis is 100 miles W of here across the Libyan Desert.

⁂

22. (31.10.16)

Same place
31.X.16

Dear Violet,
Many thanks for your last splendid long letter telling me all about your success deer-stalking.
I am glad you did so well and enjoyed Glenartney so much. It must be a ripping place.

I believe I did write and thank you for "Pip" and the other books, which I much enjoyed.
It was awfully good of you to send them.

I had quite a little success, with a portion of my "army" a short time ago when we
got altogether a bag of 196 Senussi. The C in C was very pleased with us and sent a word
of congratulation. Now the Senussi are reported to have moved right away West towards
Tripoli, so it's quite likely we shall be moved away somewhere too, but I don't know what
our destination is to be – nor whether we stay in this country or move out of it – but please
go on writing & addressing letters just the same.

I hope you won't catch cold cooking in a hot kitchen in the winter. Jolly good of you
to take it on.

You do not mention your throat, so I hope it is quite all right now – anyhow it didn't
prevent you going out deerstalking.

Major Brodie (of Brodie), my Bde Major, had a letter from his brother in France a few
days ago quoting an article from a German newspaper written by a German doctor of high
standing. In it he advocated the principle of "Hate" being fostered and encouraged and
taught to the young so as to bring it to a greater state of intensity. He finished up with the
following maxim. "Faith, Hope, and Hate these three – but the greatest of these is Hate".
Charming principles from a perfect gentleman, I don't think.

Take care of yourself.
Kindest regards to Ruckley.
Yrs very sincerely
Reginald Hoare

23. (28.11.16)

Headquarters
2nd Dismounted Bde
E. E. F.
Egypt
28.XI.16

Dear Violet,
How are you getting on with your cooking at V.A.D. Hospital. I hope you don't find it very
tiring. We have had a most enjoyable treat in a visit from Lena Ashwells Concert party,
they were 4 ladies & 2 gents, and gave us two capital open air concerts, to which 1000 men
went each time sitting on the sand of the desert. I rigged up a splendid stage for them, and it
was a beautiful still night, so we could hear perfectly. The most popular songs were "a long,
long trail", "Tennessee", "The Rag-picker", and "Pack up your troubles in an old kit bag and

Senussi prisoners under guard. (Ogilvie, *The Fife and Forfar Yeomanry and 14th (F. & F. Yeo.) Battn. R.H. 1914-1919*)

Smile, smile, smile". Do you know those?

The night after they left we actually got a shower of rain at about 7 pm, but that was all. It cleared up afterwards, & the night was quite fine. Consequently, men were rather surprised to find at mid-night a river running through their tents. There had been a "cloudburst" somewhere 20-30 miles off on the high desert, and a regular river 50 yards broad and 2 ft deep came suddenly rushing through the camp. Two of my regiments lost a lot of their clothing which was swept away before they could collect it, and our Church army Hut was washed down & the railway breached in several places. The men had to bivoac out on a dry part of the desert for the rest of the night. But there is plenty of desert, so they had not far to go.

Oddly enough it was almost the anniversary of the great storm & flood which we had at Suvla a year ago. Of course, the river had ceased to exist by the next evening, and the ground now is nearly dry again. They say they have not known such a thing for 20 years.

If any lady wants to come out to Egypt for the winter, she had better get up a Concert Party or join a theatrical party. We have now out in this country Ada Reeve's theatrical Co, and Lena Ashwell's Concert party. Officers wives are not allowed to come out. Of course, these parties are intended for the entertainment of the soldiers in the country, and are not really on a money-making expedition, but they give public performances in Cairo & Alexandria to pay their expenses.

When you have nothing else to write about, write & tell me what qualities you most admire in men, & love in women. There's a conundrum for you which will make you think. When I get your answer (which must be absolutely impartial) I will send you my answer to the same.

An "enemy aeroplane" suddenly arrived over Cairo last week and dropped a few bombs but did very little damage.

I hope you have managed to put in a few days hunting & have been well carried & had some sport. I wonder when I shall see hounds again.

My best wishes to you all for a Happy Xmas, and I hope the war will be over before Xmas 1917.

Yours very sincerely
Reginald Hoare

---

24. (10.12.16)

2nd Dismounted Me
E. E. F.
10.XII.16

Dear Violet,
I think this should reach you about Xmas, so I send my best wishes to you all for this (usually) festive season, & I hope you are all going very strong.

I am so sorry Monica had to have an operation for Appendicitis. How very wise of her to have it when she was really well. I hope she has quite recovered, & that you too feel no ill effects from your throat now that the winter has come with its damp & snow.

I am writing this near the shores of Lake Timsah, Ismailia, and we get plenty of sunshine here. The men bathe daily in the Suez Canal or in this Lake, but I've not had time to go for a dip yet.

If the Censor opens this letter, I expect he will put his blue pencil through the foregoing information; but I think the Turks must know we have some troops at Ismailia.

I spent most of yesterday going round some of the canal defence works in a motor car; it was very interesting, and I quite expect I shall spend my Xmas here, or hereabouts.

I spent last Xmas on a transport in Mudros Harbour just after the evacuation of the Gallipoli peninsula. I wonder where I shall spend next Xmas.

I hope you are getting on well with your cooking at the V.A.D and have not given any of the patients a pain in the "middle of the "Knight", by your culinary efforts. One of my sisters cleans and trims 22 lamps at a V.A.D. Hospital. Ugh. I do not like handling parrafin lamps, do you?

Now I must stop this as I am going off to a school of Instruction near Cairo for a "Senior Officers course" to get all the latest hints and tips, as to "How to kill Huns". I have volunteered for it. It's a nice time of life to go to school, but one is a schoolboy all one's life in the Army.

All sorts of good wishes to you all for Xmas & the coming New Year, and I hope 1917 will see the world at peace & happier.

Yours very sincerely
Reginald Hoare

Unloading horses at Suez.

25. (20.12.16)

2nd Dismounted Bde
E. E. F.
Dec 20th

Dear Violet,

Ever so many thanks for your last two splendid long letters. You have been <u>awfully</u> good about writing to me, and I find your letters most interesting.

So glad to hear Monica has got over her operation so well, but I expect she still feels the effect of it this cold weather and will have to be careful, for some time yet.

Many thanks for sending me the "Eve" book, and the nice soap. Both kind thoughts. I have read some of "Eve's" letters and they are quite amusing. I am also very fond of nice soap; aren't you? And I like people who look clean and "bien soigné"; don't you?

Many thanks for your good wishes for Xmas. The same to all of you, and many of them.

Last Xmas I spent at sea – or rather on a transport in Mudros Harbour – We transshipped from one transport from Imbros onto another in Mudros Harbour on Xmas morning. This Xmas I look like spending on dry land – very dry land. Much drier than you have at home, or the poor fellows have in Flanders. I am writing this near Ismailia on the Suez Canal, but if the Censor opens this letter, he will probably put his blue pencil through that piece of information.

But wherever we move to the Military Postal authorities <u>out here</u> are let into the secret, so letters and parcels are always forwarded very quickly from the Base post office.

I hope you are none the worse for the wetting you got when "Pinkie" elected to dive and swim the river, instead of walking quietly through it. The death by drowning of the runaway horse was most tragic, and I am sorry that your good nature in stopping to hold other horses, should have lost you the end of the hunt. But there always is some satisfaction in knowing one has done a kind action. Don't you think so?

I think death by drowning is quite a fitting fate for a beastly horse that ran away with you & Monica and the young soldier man, and the owner is jolly lucky not to have been the cause of severe injuries to you. I have no use for a man who lends or lets out an unsafe animal for ladies to ride. (There's a "strafe" for you. I hope the owner of the horse is not a great friend of yours).

I hope the photos you are having taken will turn out well, & that I shall be sent one as a New Year's card. I hope your father has got over his influenza cold & that his eye has quite recovered.

I had some capital lawn tennis on the hard courts at the Club in Ismalia this afternoon, which I much enjoyed. The boogumvillea, Irgnonea and pointsettias are a blaze of colour in the gardens, but the colours "swear" at each other dreadfully.

I don't know whether I've spelt these blooming flowers' names correctly. They do fairly bloom here. The weather has been perfect lately – Very little wind – just a very gentle breeze. Rather "chillsome" in the early morning in a tent, temperature at 6 AM about 46, but glorious sunshine most of the day.

We are camped on the desert sand near the shores of Lake Timsah. I live in a tent but dine in a matting hut.

I don't think your hospital pass entitles you to half fare all over the world. I think it only entitles you to half fare when in uniform and travelling on duty. But I'm not quite sure. Yes, the Senusi are very quiet now, and I think have found that fighting doesn't pay.

The Nile at this time of year, and always, is dirty. Gorgeous sunsets – yes, and at a distance, with the sun on it, it looks clean; but if you get near you will find it very dirty & brown in colour; and men are forbidden either to drink it or bathe in it. To do so will give you a horrid illness called "Bilhartzia", which the men call "Billy 'Arris".

Lots more good wishes to you all for the New Year, and I hope you'll have some good sport out hunting, & no accidents.

Yrs v. sincerely Reginald Hoare.

P.S. If any lady wants to come out to Egypt. I think her best chance now would be to come in charge of performing fleas, or as a performer on the slack wire. Something to amuse the soldiers. No ordinary lady is allowed out here, but theatrical companies and concert parties are allowed to come. I think perhaps these latter have got a bit common now, and your best chance, if you want to come out, is as a performer on the slack wire. Perhaps Monica, after her operation, is more fitted for a less active part, and might come in charge of performing fleas. Walk up for the "Sisters Walker".

What rot I am writing. I shall stop. A Happy New Year to you all.

27. (24.1.17)

Headquarters
This is the new title of my old Brigade
229th Infantry Bde
24.1.17

Dear Violet,

Many thanks for your long letter of Jan 7th, I am so glad to hear my Xmas letter & New Year card were so nicely timed, and actually arrived on the right day. That was a wonderful piece of management, yet I assure you I did not charter a special ship, nor engage a special train for them. It was just luck.

I have moved again since I last wrote, & unless the Censor opens the letter & "blue pencils" the information, you may like to know that I am now on the banks of the Suez Canal at EL FERDAN, a few miles N of Ismailia, & have made my headquarters in the only block of buildings in the place, belonging to the Canal Co. Ships pass within 50 yards of my window, but as most of them pass during the night, I don't see very much of them.

I've just come back from a trip to El Arish – thats further off East, & on the coast. A L.&S.W.Ry Engine pulled the train along, and it was a very interesting trip.

Alongside of the line is a wire netting track for 80 or 90 miles for the infantry to march along, as its very tiring & slow work marching in heavy sand. The wire netting makes quite good "going", but of course Cavalry, Guns, or vehicles are not allowed to use it, or they would soon ruin it.

I was within 20 miles of the scenes of the two recent fights but got there too late to *see* anything of them, but heard that the Worcester, Warwickshire & Gloster Yeomanry did very well.

The infantry out there are also being fitted out with sand-sandals, made of stout wire netting, to tie on over their boots, like snow shoes, with leather thongs. (Picture of shoe) I tried a pair of them on and found I could run about in the soft desert sand like anything without sinking in or slipping back. (The above drawing is not that of a beetle, but a sand-sandal.) The Artillery wheels are all fitted with "ped-rails" and require teams of 14 horses to draw them through the sand. What would Gwynne think of that – 14 horses instead of 6?

I am sorry to hear your father is threatened with appendicitis again. I hope its only a false alarm, the result of plum pudding & mince pies at Xmas. I can quite understand your finding the big cauldrons & pots too heavy for you at this hospital.

So glad to hear you've enjoyed some good hunts, and that Pinkie took care of you. Ismailia can be pronounced either way, but I believe "Ismyleer" is correct.

Mail just going. Kindest regards to you all.

Yrs very sincerely
Reginald Hoare.

We saw a fox on the desert two mornings ago & made hunting noises & galloped after it, but we lost it.

28. (10.2.17)

New title of my old Brigade 229th Inf. Bde
E.E.F.
10.2.17

Dear Violet,

Thanks <u>awfully</u> for the charming photo of yourself, the socks & letter. I like the photo <u>very</u> much. I think it is a very good one of you, and you are looking very merry & bright, with "some" smile. You have evidently learned to "pack up your troubles in an old kit bag, and smile, smile, smile", as the song sung by the men goes. Do you know that song?

I don't think the hands are "awful" at all. Very nice hands. But the left one is in an odd position, that's all. The socks are a capital fit. What a good shot you made at it – and nice soft wool. I believe I buy 10 1/2 in socks always to allow for shrinking.

I am very sorry the letter you wrote answering my conundrums went to the bottom of the sea. Never mind, try again. The conundrum is, what qualities do you most admire in a man, & love in a woman? When I get your answer, I will send you mine.

No, I was not taking any part in the El Arish fight, but I went up there a fortnight ago to have a look at the place and stayed a couple of days with the General in Command of the Desert Column, and it was a very interesting trip. I can well understand how anxious you must be with Gwynne up in the Somme sector, and I hope he will manage to keep out of harm's way for all your sakes.

Here our life has lately been uneventful, and without excitement. The nearest we have been to any excitement was the receipt of a wire saying two enemy aeroplanes were flying our way, but they never came over here.

We had a scratch game of polo on the desert last Saturday but have been unable to find any place where the sand is firm enough to make a decent ground. It is all very soft sand round here, and the ball soon gets buried, & we have to hack and hack at it to get it out. But its good fun and good exercise, and one cannot be particular in wartime.

I hope your father's threat of appendicitis is now quite exploded, and that he is quite fit again.

What do you think of the Bosches' threat of increased frightfulness and activity in his submarine campaign? Personally, I don't see how he can do any more than he has been doing. He has been doing his worst for some time, but his new submarines may be bigger & better than his old ones. Let's hope he is losing them as fast as he turns them out.

So, you don't think you'd be any good on the slack wire? Try performing dogs. I don't like the idea of you as a cook. I am sure you would scorch your face at the fire & spoil your nice hands. I am so glad the photo did not go to the bottom of the sea, along with your other letter, and I am sorry I have missed getting that.

I say, Violet, why shouldn't you write to me, and address me as Reggie, instead of the very formal "Dear Gen: H". Please do, <u>if you'd like to;</u> being addressed as "Gen" makes me feel <u>so</u> old. But I have been told the Subalterns say I'm not a bit like a General, and I certainly don't feel old enough to be one.

So glad the new pony has turned out such a flyer – or is it flier? Take care of yourself and mind the corners.

Kind regards to you all.

Yours very sincerely

Reginald Hoare

I don't feel that I've thanked you half enough for the photo & socks.

—————

29. (25.2.17)

229th Inf Bde
Feb 25th

Dear Violet,

I enclose some seeds of the Egyptian Loophar – the thing you use in your bath – which you may like to try. I got them from the wall of a small house near here. The Loophar is a <u>creeper</u> which grows to a goodish height, & the Loophar itself hangs down like an enormous pod, in shape & size like a banana, only about 3 times as big. When absolutely bone dry, the loophar has to be peeled & cut open & the seeds removed before it can be used. <u>Sow in sandy soil.</u> I wonder if these will produce loophars which will be absolutely bone dry before the war is over. Of course, you will have to grow these under glass, as they would never stand cold & damp.

I played polo on the desert yesterday afternoon. Such a ground. We just take out some signalling flags for goal posts & put them down on any open smooth bit of the desert which is free or fairly free from stones & bushes. Of course, the ground soon gets cut up, & the ball gets buried in the sand; but we seldom play on the same ground twice. There is plenty of desert to choose from, but it's not easy to find a good piece fit for polo.

Look here; when you have answered my conundrums about the qualities which you most <u>admire</u> in man or woman, then let me know what you most <u>dislike</u> in man or woman.

We have had hotter weather the last two or three days lately. I hope you are getting better weather now and are not snowed up.

How is Monica? And does she work for the Red X or munitions? I have two nieces in France, one works in a gas helmet factory, and the other in a hospital.

No hunting for you lately, so Pinkie will be very fresh when you next hunt him. Kindest regards to you all, & I hope Gwynne keeps merry & bright.

Yours very sincerely

Reginald Hoare

I hate these writing blocks, but I've got no other paper.

—————

30. (16.3.17)

229th Inf: Bde
E.E.F.
16.3.17

Dear Violet,

Many thanks for your letter of Feb 21st.

I am so sorry to hear you have got to have another operation for your tonsil. It must be very disappointing to you, and you have all my sympathy, as I can well imagine how you must dread it. But I often think that sort of thing is far worse in the expectation than in the realization.

I hope by the time this reaches you that the operation is over, that it wasn't <u>nearly</u> as bad as you thought it would be, and that you are now free from pain and discomfort & feeling <u>ever</u> so much better for it.

Here we are at El Arish, and its certainly a more interesting place as we get frequent visits from "Fritz", who flies over us 2 or 3 mornings a week and gives our anti-aircraft guns some fire practise at "rocketters". They have not succeeded in bringing Fritz down yet, but I am sure they have scared him. Like the Irish Keeper said to encourage the sportsman who always missed every snipe, "Begorra, Captain, but you made him leave the place anyhow."

I am sorry to hear Gwynne has "gone sick", but I hope he will soon pull round at Mentone. It is such a pretty place, and very nice at this time of year. I hope Mon: is keeping fit, and as you don't mention your father, I imagine the appendicitis scare *was* only a scare, & that he keeps "out and about", and will soon be wanting you "in brass buttons and a top-hat" – (I suppose you mean in <u>a coat</u> with brass-buttons. Brass buttons by themselves would be rather chilly for the time of year) to drive him to the station when the petrol allowance stops.

I heard an amusing story about a certain General in France yesterday. He was given to being rather theatrical in his manner and was somewhat of a "poseur" and pompous. He was going round inspecting his men in the trenches one morning, and one of the men had managed to get hold of more rum than was good for him, so his comrades rolled him up in a blanket, & hid him away in a corner to sleep it off. But the General spotted him, and seeing he was rolled up in a blanket, thought it was a dead man who had been shot by a sniper. So, he halted in front of "the corpse", drew himself up to attention, and in a theatrical manner saluted "the corpse", saying, "I Adolphus, Christopher Robinson salute my dead hero". A voice from inside the blanket was heard to say in beery tones "Whatsh that the old fool is shaying about me?" Then the row began.

Isn't the news about Baghdad splendid, and all the news from France too is very good. I think the Turk is in a bad way all round and if he isn't careful he'll get another nasty knock from this side before long, and I think he will shortly sue for a separate peace.

We are camped about half a mile from the sea, & men bathe daily. Our camp is among fig trees, which are planted all round El Arish like a sort of fig tree orchard, only the trees are very wide apart & much scattered. The leaf on them is just coming out, and they smell very "figgy" in the early morning when the sun gets on them after a heavy dew or rain.

We have had some very heavy rain, but today has been perfect. And we have had some vile dust storms with high wind which makes life in a tent very unpleasant, with sand flying about all over the place.

I sincerely hope this will find you convalescent & comfortable. Take care of yourself, & mind you don't catch cold.

Kindest regards to you all.

Yrs v. sincerely

Reginald Hoare

⚬⚬⚬

31. (5.4.17)

60 miles from Jerusalem.
5.4.17

Dear Violet,

I am so glad to get your letter of March 18th to find that you have made such a splendid recovery. Well done you. And I hope you will go ahead fast now and derive a lasting benefit from the last operation. Fancy you being well enough to go out hunting again so soon. That shows you have jolly good "recuperative powers". Well, here I am 13 miles from GAZA where the last fight was, & move forward a bit nearer that place tomorrow.

You must watch the papers for the account of the next fight, when we hope to knock Johnny Turk off his perch for good and all.

The place I am close to is supposed to be the birthplace of Delilah, but I have seen no Delilahs about, only a lot of ugly old hags.

We are separated from the sea by a belt of sandhills 150-250 feet high, & about a mile wide, & inland of them the country is gently undulating, (without trees), with crops of barley, vetch, and grass growing on a very sandy soil, which quickly breaks up.

Round the towns & villages are orchards or gardens, divided up by unpenetrable [sic] fences of cactus & prickly pear. In the gardens are Apricot trees, almond trees and what look like peach trees and pomegranate trees, all sadly needing pruning, & now smothered with dust, as the soil quickly breaks up.

We get a few Jaffa oranges here, but they come by camel convoys from Jaffa & are not from here – I expect a good few Turkish spies come along with them. Many thanks for the answers to my conundrums. I like them. – especially punctuality in a woman. That often is caused by selfishness & a want of consideration for others, don't you think? I put manliness in a man, and womanliness in a woman first of all – an effeminate man or a "mannish" woman are not to my liking, but I do admire a sporting woman, or one who takes an interest in sport. She can be sporting without being "mannish" by which I mean trying to "ape" a man too much.

I <u>admire</u> a woman who is well turned out, does her hair well, has generally a "bien soigneé" appearance, without being over dressed in any way. "Puts her clothes on well" expresses it, and a woman who does that seldom has an untidy head of hair. Neatness & tidyness in a woman are attractive qualities. I heard a man once say of a woman. "A nice woman – very- but I wish someone would give her a piece of soap and a toothbrush." Very cynical, but I think both a man and a woman lose a lot of their attractiveness if they are not cleanly in their appearance. Sympathetic, good tempered, good natured, and to be good company are all valuable attributes, but there is no such thing as perfection in human nature.

I am writing this in camp by the light of one candle, & I hope you will be able to read it. Please excuse pencil – it is so much less trouble than ink in camp, & ink is rather precious.

I hope you will finish the season well, & that you & Monica will enjoy some good hunts. I wonder when I shall be hunting a fox instead of a Turk.

I hope the Loophar seeds are behaving nicely – You should sell some of them for the Red X fund at the next bazaar.

I hope you all keep fit & well & are not feeling the shortage of sugar.

Kindest regards to you all

Yrs very sincerely

Reginald Hoare

32. (10.5.17)

(In the Outport Line)
229th Inf Bde
May 10th

Dear Violet,

It seems quite a long time since I heard from you, and I hope all is well, & that you have finished the hunting season with some good gallops, been well carried, & kept free from accidents.

Here we are shelling the Turk, & the Turk shells us daily. It quite reminds me of old times on the Gallipoli Peninsular, only that we have plenty of room to move about in.

My "little lot" took no very active part in the recent operations near GAZA, as we were in reserve, but still we had 15 casualties, all caused by shell fire. We get a steady dribble of deserters from the Turks. Yesterday I got two and 5 more this morning, so I don't think they are enjoying life, while we keep "merry & bright. Cheerio."

A good story is told of an Australian who was in charge of an escort to 146 Turkish prisoners, taken in the recent operations, & which he had to conduct back to the Prisoners Camp, (which had been prepared from them). He was asked if he could conduct them back by night & replied "Lor. Yes. I'm used to driving cattle through the bush by night." However, when the morning came, he counted heads, & found that he had only got 145. He had allowed one to escape. His reputation was at stake. Was he downhearted? No. He saw an old Bedouin working on his farm, so he rounded him up, put him in the bag, & handed in 146 prisoners "all correct". I cannot promise you that the story is a true one, but it's very typical of the Australians. They are never at a loss for "a way out" of a difficulty.

The flies are very bad here now, & I've paused several times in this letter to kill a few dozens, with a wire gauze "fly swatter" – a very deadly instrument, and if you'd like to be very kind, you may send me a couple of them, and another piece of the nice Violet soap. I also killed a yellow scorpion in my writing case, when I opened it to get this paper out. The plagues of Egypt.

The news from France is splendid, and I hope it's the beginning of the end of this horrid war. I trust you get good accounts from Gwynne, and that he is making a good bag with his guns.

We had a hot wave last week When for 3 days the temperature went up to 112 in the shade, but its nice & cool again now, & about 80 in my tent as I write.

Kindest regards to you all.

Yrs v. sincerely

Reginald Hoare

⚜

33. (2.6.17)

In the trenches –
229th Inf Bde, E.E.F.
2.6.17

Dear Violet,

Here we are in the month of June – "June the month of Roses – I wonder if you have got 'Roses, Roses all the way'". I am so fond of Roses; aren't you?

Many thanks for your last letter of April 29th.

I am so glad to hear you finished the hunting season with a good 50 minutes on your last day, and "negotiated" the big stake & bound fence with a wide brook on the landing side in safety and enjoyed yourself no end after that. I wish I'd been there. I can't help being amused about the meatless day in London. The same thing happened to my sister – got up early in the country; & went to London for the day. After a hard mornings shopping, arrived V. hungry to lunch at the Cavalry Club, & found it a meatless day there. Got home to a meatless dinner. We never have a meatless day out here – there is always "Bully Beef" when we don't get fresh meat, and potatoes 3 or 4 times a week – I believe they come from

Turkish prisoners.

Cyprus. The troops really are extraordinarily well fed.

I think the Turks were celebrating a birthday one day last week – or else the Sultan's favourite wife had presented him with twin sons. Anyhow he suddenly began to bombard us with his Artillery at 2 AM firing "salvos" – ie. all guns at once. This lasted for ten minutes. Then he began again at 3.30 AM, same thing; and finally recommenced at 4.30 AM and bombarded us for half an hour.

I suppose he thought he was killing scores of us, but I am thankful to say my casualties were only 5 wounded – and 2 of those were caused by the men coming out of their "dug-outs" too soon without an order. They made sure that the bombardment would be followed by an attack and wanted to get ready for it – but nothing more happened – 1200 shells are reckoned to have been fired. We have occasional night skirmishes with the Turks, and one of my parties had quite a sharp engagement with some last night and managed to "lay out" some of them.

Sorry to see Invincible did not acquit himself better in the 2000 gs, but if – as the papers said – he had had a hurried preparation he certainly ran as well as could be expected. Better luck next time.

So you confess to finding it difficult to be punctual. Well, I think there are times when unpunctuality doesn't matter, that is when no one else is inconvenienced by it – But there are times when it matters a great deal. I know a lady who is quite impossible to ask to join a dinner & theatre prty. She is always 20 min: to half an hour late to the dinner, & so one misses a lot of the play & other people have to suffer in consequence. The great thing is to start dressing – or whatever it is – in good time. (This reads almost like a lecture for you. but I don't mean it to be). Personally, I hate getting behind hand with anything – Time flies, & one never can catch up lost minutes. I suppose as a soldier one learns to be punctual – with exceptions.

Anyhow once one has got into the habit of it, it's no trouble, and <u>not half the effort</u> of having to put on speed because one knows ones late.

We get a lovely breeze off the sea from the tops of the hills round here which is very cooling in the afternoon. Up to now this climate of the land of the Philistines is far nicer than the climate of the Nile Valley. It was <u>terribly hot at Gaza last May. I suppose we shall get it hotter here before long</u>.

Haven't the Italians done <u>splendidly</u> lately. And I expect before long we shall hear of the Russians making a big move – wait & see. And I hear we are doing quite well with the U-boats & getting quite a lot of them. I really believe it's the beginning of the end. Stick to it. "It's dogged does it".

Please remember me to Mon, & all at Ruckley, & do write again. I like hearing from you.
Yrs v. sincerely
Reginald Hoare
I hope you get good accounts of Gwynne.

34. (20.6.17)

229th Inf: Brigade
E.E.F.
20.6.17

Dear Violet,

So very sorry to hear Gwynne has been wounded, but I am very glad to learn from your letter that they have got him home and that he is going on well. It must be a great relief to you all that things are no worse. I hope he will make a good recovery and come out of it quite sound.

I saw the announcement of your uncle Roylance Court's death[4] in the papers, and I am sure you will all miss him very much. Accept my sincere sympathy. What a splendid sportsman he was.

So, you complain that you haven't had a letter from me for a long time. I like that sort of complaint from you. But perhaps some of my letters have gone down to the watery depths "below, below, below", as these beastly submarines have sunk a mail or two lately. We are told we shall only get one mail a fortnight from England, so I shall complain if I don't get a letter from you soon.

We keep hammering away at the Turks, and last week the Brigade on my left captured & raided one of their posts and bagged the garrison of it – only one escaped. Deserters from the Turks continue to dribble in, & they are "fed up" with getting lots of digging to do, & little to eat & drink. I don't think the deserters are samples of their best material, though occasionally an officer comes & surrenders. One prisoner said the Turks knew we were not really fighting against them, but against the Germans. He said a lot of them wanted to come and surrender, but they did not know how to do it. One cannot believe quite all that a discontented soldier says.

The Turks' anti-aircraft guns – with Austrian or German gunners – give our aeroplanes a hot time of it, and I am always much relieved when our flying men get out of shot.

My night patrols have some exciting incidents when they lie out to try & catch Turkish patrols, and occasionally they bag a few. But the Turk is more given to throwing a bomb and running away than putting up a stand-up fight – and he can run very fast.

I am glad to hear the loophar seeds are promising, but I don't understand your gardener thinking they want so much water. I should try some with plenty of water, & some kept on the dry side, & see which does best.

I live in my shirt sleeves, & my face, hands & arms are burnt to a regular copper colour, as I generally ride about or walk about with my shirt sleeves turned up. Most of the men strip to the waist when off duty – especially if their shirt is being washed & dried.

We have some hot days, but nothing compared to the heat at Gaza this time last year. There is a lovely cool breeze off the sea this afternoon, and I should love to go and have a bathe but its 3 miles off.

I am told the men on the Stock Exchange are betting 10 to 1 on the war being over this Autumn. I only hope that may be so. But personally, I do not expect to get home for any grouse shooting this year. How are the grouse at Cabrach? Have you had any reports from there yet.

---

4   Died 18/5/1917. Married 17/1/1883 Mary Carlaw Walker 20/3/1858–17/12/1933, elder daughter and 4th of the 8 children of Sir Andrew Barclay Walker.

I am afraid your father is very disappointed at his Invincible not getting another chance of showing his real merit, but if conditions improve I quite expect racing will be started again & let's hope he will win the Leger in the Autumn.

Tell Gwynne to keep his tail cocked. I hope he is not suffering much, & that we shall soon hear his cheery whistle about on the moor again.

Kindest regards to you all, & I hope Mon is having a good time in Hampshire.

Yours v. sincerely

Reginald Hoare

---

35. (9.7.17)

229th Inf.: Bde
E.E.F.
9.7.17

Dear Violet,

You are a dear to have sent me some more of that beautiful Violet soap, and the fly killers. They arrived safely this morning, & I have just unpacked them. I could not imagine what "clothing" you could be sending me in July. The fly killers are quite the right kind, but we have so "strafed" the flies that we have reduced their nuisance to an absolute minimum.

I am so glad to hear Gwynne has made such a good recovery, and that you and Monica were able to enjoy a play with him. It's a long time since I saw any plays but let's hope this Russian advance which has begun with such a good success will mean the beginning of the end of the War and of the Huns, and that before another year is out we may be seeing a play together.

So glad to hear of "Florinets" success in Ireland, and I hope "Invincible" may get a chance of proving the good horse I feel sure he is, before the year is over.

The Turks opposite us have been very quiet lately; I think their artillery must be saving up their ammunition for a big "splash" later on, as their guns fire very little, and we give them 50 shells for everyone they fire at us.

I killed a big black snake in the trenches a few evenings ago, and one of my officers killed 3 in one day in the trenches.

Yes, it's a good deal hotter now, and the ground looks dreadfully dried up, & is no longer the rolling green downland it was when we first got up here. No rain is expected before November. I had a visit from the new Commander in Chief a few days ago, when he came round my trenches, & was very pleased at all he saw. I also did showman to a party of French officers who came to admire the view towards Jerusalem & Beersheba from my frontline trenches.

I think it's quite likely some of my letters & some of yours may be at the bottom of the sea. But you have been awfully good about writing, and I am sure you are kept busy with your V.A.D. work and that it's not easy to find the time to write letters. Besides there are others to write to. I think it's wonderful Capt. Bewicke riding and winning a race at his age. He is a marvel.[5]

---

5   Captain Perceval Wentworth Bewicke (1861-1950): Renowned for his performance upon the turf, he was
    a champion amateur jockey in 1891-92 and 1894 respectively. One notable win was the Grand Military

We have been in these trenches now a long time and are moving back tonight for a rest & change. I don't expect it will be much of a rest as we shall be kept drilling and training, but it will be a change from the trenches. My nephew out here who has been in command of a Battery R.H.A.[6] has got the Military Cross, at which I am much pleased. He has not been under my command, so I had nothing to do with his being recommended for it, but I heard from his General that he had done a lot of real hard and good work.

Now I must stop this. Kindest regards to you all, and <u>ever</u> so many more thanks for the soap etc.

Yrs v. sincerely

Reginald Hoare

Have you heard any report of the grouse yet this year? And will you go to Cabrach to shoot or elsewhere?

☙ ❧

36. (23.7.17)

Savoy Palace Hotel
Alexandrie
Egypt
July 23rd

Dear Violet,

Many thanks for your last letter written from Manfair Rectory. I forget whether I met Mrs Crawshay at Ruckley or not. I hope the change & rest from the Hospital work did you good.

I am here on a few days leave too for a change, and to do some shopping, & visit the dentist. He was very kind to me, & found next to nothing to do, I am glad to say.

It's very hot & moist here, and I am just going off to San Stephano for a bathe in the Sea. I have had two bathes there since I got here. I tried to get rooms at the Casino Hotel at that place, which is a suburb of Alexandria, & right on the sea, but it was packed though it has 700 bedrooms. This Hotel too is quite full, & my nephew had to sleep on the floor last night. It is holiday time just now for the natives, and they all flock to Alexandria.

It took me 26 hours to get here from "the front", and I go back there tomorrow morning.

Your father will be pleased at 40 more days racing being allowed. Ask him if he ever received a letter from me months ago containing a cheque for a "bit" on "Invincible" when he was to be "expected". I am afraid that letter has gone to the bottom of the deep blue sea, & I've never heard from your father.

I went to the races here on Saturday, and managed to back one winner, but was a loser on the day.

Now I must stop this, and go and have a look at the polo, & then have my last bathe before returning to our "dust-heap" at the front.

I hope Gwynne is mending up well.

Yrs very sincerely

Reginald Hoare

---

on Ormerod in 1892.

6   RH's nephew is mentioned several times in the correspondence but remains unidentified with certainty at time of going to press. Apparently those interred at Kham Yunus (see letter 38) were relocated after the war.

Brigadier-General Reginald Hoare, Egypt c. 1917.

37. (12.8.17)

229th Inf Bde
Aug 12th

Dear Violet,

I wonder if you are all up at Cabrach, or where you are. Perhaps your father will have taken another place again this year. But I hear there is some difficulty in getting sporting cartridge, though the breed? of rifle cartridges, & shells is very plentiful.

I don't suppose I shall see a grouses's feather this year but perhaps in another two or 3 years (!) when the war is over I shall hear the old cockbird saying "go back, go back, go back" once more. But I really think the Hun is on his last legs now, though his last legs may continue to carry him for some time yet.

I am writing this from our new camp which is about a mile from the sea, but separated from it by heavy, soft sand dunes, so that mile is worse than 2 miles of good going and will rather choke the men off from going for a bathe. We are also kept hard at work training our men how to defeat "Johnny" Turk, so get very few opportunities of getting a bathe.

I am living in a little rush hut which hardly keeps the sun out, and certainly would not keep the rain out, but we've had no rain since February, and don't expect any for another month. It's still very hot, but my rush hut is airy & lets the breeze through everywhere. It is a delightful climate for sitting about under a shady tree or verandah & reading a book but when all one's work has to be done out in the sun daily, the heat is rather trying. It's generally over 80 in the shade by 8AM & anything you like in the sun. There are a lot of fig trees in our camp, & plenty of figs on them, but wretched little small things & the trees look very neglected as if they wanted pruning badly. How they grow in this sand beats me, but I expect their roots get down to water, & the most wonderful thing about this place is that you can get water by digging down 3 to 5 ft among these sand dunes, & even right on the beach for miles along the coast – and good fresh water too. How are my "loophars" looking now? I wonder if they will grow any "fruit" this year.

I wonder if you go to Cabrach who your guns will be. I hope Gwynne will be well enough to shoot & that your father will find his cartridges as straight as ever.

You & Monica must try and get a few more birds between you. Do you remember when you arrived at the Buck with one grouse, which the dog had caught. But you shot one afterwards in my butt, & I hope you'll shoot many more.

Kindest remembrances to you all, & best wishes for "Invincible" & the rest of the stable.
Yrs v. sincerely
Reginald Hoare

38. (22.8.17)

229th Inf: Bde
E. E. F.
Egypt
Aug 22nd

Dear Violet,
Many thanks for your last letter of July 24th, which arrived just as I had written to you.

Your last letter told me all about the great interest and excitement in "Invincible's" chance for the Derby. I hope you got away to Cambridge & were able to see the race, but I am sorry you did not see him win. Where did you stay at Cambridge? Have you been to Newmarket before? I like Newmarket very much, but I like all race meetings least when there is a crowd.

So. you have been bathing in the bathing pool. Well, I rode down to the sea, tied my horse up to a post, and had a glorious bathe this morning. The water was beautifully warm, & it was most enjoyable. The bathing however is considered rather dangerous, & even strong swimmers are cautioned not to go out beyond their waists, as the tide & "under-tow" is very strong. One Australian clad in a slouch hat & shrimping net was a picturesque sight. He was as brown as a berry all over, like most of our men who are only half clad when off duty in the daytime. I saw two more Australians throw bombs into the sea, and then when they exploded, they swam out & dived about like porpoises to see if they could find any dead fish, killed by the explosion. I saw one of them hold up one fish about the size of a herring. Of course, they are not allowed to use bombs for killing fish with, but the Australians are not famous for strict adherence to the regulations.

Beside the bathing place in the sea, we have washing places nearer camp, where men can obtain fresh water, and have a shower bath; The Shower bath consists of an empty petrol tin hung up from a high tripod of poles, & it is filled by a pump and hose from a

water-hole. (See drawing.) Here you see it. The little figures represent naked men who have had their soap once at a trough in the distance (not in the sketch) and are waiting their turn for a "shower". On the right is a naked man (with a helmet on) pumping for his pals. They all take a turn to pump for each other to fill the petrol tin with water, it has fine holes punched in the bottom of it which makes a beautiful "shower". It is an amusing scene. Men wear very few clothes out here when off duty. There are <u>never</u> any ladies about, so it does not matter how often they wear their "birthday suit" besides it gives them a chance of washing their "undies".

I am off to ride to Kham Yunus this afternoon to see my nephew's[7] grave there. He was killed in the first battle of Gaza. I say! I think it's time you sent me another snapshot of yourself in your everyday out of door clothes. Will you please? The green figs are very good here now and are a real treat. They grow all round my "hutch".

We have lizards, chameleons, scorpions and centipedes for company here, but only chameleons as pets; the two latter insects are <u>pests</u>, though they have never troubled me.

Please notice in the sketch that like all famous artists, I have put my initials and date to the picture.

I hope you are going strong & that before long "Invincible" will cover himself with glory by winning in good company.

Now I must stop, as my horses are waiting. I wish you were <u>going</u> to ride with me. Do you remember our ride together & the "leps" we took?

Yrs. v. sincerely
Reginald Hoare

⁓◉ ◉⁓

39. (7.9.17)

Headquarters
229th Inf Bde
7.9.17

Dear Violet,
I wonder how many grouse you have shot at Cabrach or elsewhere by this time. I see the report on the Moors is that the grouse in Aberdeenshire are good, so I hope your father has been enjoying some good sport and was catching the birds just under the chin in his usual deadly method.

My Brigade have been having rather a rough time of it lately, as we were lent to another Division to dig a new advanced line of trenches for them in "no – man's land". Of course,

---

7   This would be his niece Muriel's husband, Capt Robert Egerton Loder, 1887 – died of wounds 29/3/1917, Machine gun officer Royal Sussex Regt.

the digging was done by night, but the nights have been bright moonlight and as the trenches had to be dug among sand dunes, the men "showed up" very plainly against the nearly white sand.

I had 25 casualties one night, when I lost one officer killed, and I had 10 casualties another night. But my men stick to their work splendidly and dug away with the most determined manner, in spite of machine gun and artillery fire.

I got a very nice letter of thanks & praise for the way my men worked under fire. It's one thing to be brave when you are attacking, and your blood is up & you can "hit back". It's another thing to dig and suffer casualties when you can't hit back & can only shake your shovel at the enemy who is shooting at you.

However, the Turks got a bit too venturesome on the 2nd night, and we took toll of them, I think they must have suffered 100 casualties, as they were still taking away their dead and wounded at dawn. The last night my men dug & finished their task, and the Turks has evidently learnt a lesson, as they left us entirely alone without coming out & firing a single shot at us.

We were then in bivouac close to the sea, & my dugout was within 25 yards of it, so I walked out every morning, and had a ripping bathe at 6.30 AM. It was most enjoyable, except when there was a big swell on, which made the breakers rather heavy, and the bathing a bit boisterous. The tide too runs very strong on this coast, so one has to be very careful, & not too venturesome. The water was quite warm, and if the morning was at all cool, it was warmer in the water than out.

Last week two Turkish officers surrendered "complete with their servants". One of them was said to be in command of a Batt" & is <u>reported</u> to have expressed regret that he was unable to bring his Battalion along with him, but only just failed to do so. It is said that they know & feel that they are fighting for the Germans & not for themselves & they resent it. Quite right too.

I hope you are all fit & well & enjoying life.

Yrs v. sincerely

Reginald Hoare

<hr>

40.(15.9.17)

229" Inf Bde
E.E.F.
Sept 15th

Dear Violet,

Many thanks for your last letter of Aug 24th, and the beautiful pair of socks which arrived today, curiously enough within 3 days of my birthday.

That was very clever of you and very thoughtful to send me such a nice useful present.

I hope you are getting good sport with the grouse. The only grouse we see out here are a few Sandgrouse. But quail are coming in, and I hear the R.F.C. here caught 94 a few nights ago by putting up high nets along the beach. How kind of the Duke giving you all that shooting. I hope you will find the birds plentiful up there, but I expect you'd sooner see them plentiful on your own moor.

Well done Inversnaid. I saw she had won. So glad you all had a nice win. No, you cannot believe the Turkish accounts of their doings. I think they are put in the papers by a German agency by German officers.

You might have noticed in the papers of Sept 1st that we had advanced our line near Gaza. That was done by my Brigade, digging by night in bright moonlight, and it cost me 36 casualties altogether, including 1 officer killed, but we dug a trench 1400 yards long in full view of the Turks. I got such a nice letter from my superior general about the splendid determination which my men had shown in sticking to their task in spite [sic] of M.G. guns & Artillery fire. The Turks made a sort of attack on us one night while digging, & we think we inflicted 100 casualties on them, as they were seen still picking up their dead and wounded when daylight came. There is only one good kind of Bosch – or Turk – And that is a dead one. There's a bloodthirsty sentiment for you.

How I would like to join you at Cabrach. I wonder when I shall lef off my "fowling piece" at grouse again. But my place is here, though I can help others to get home on leave, if they have very strong reasons for wanting to go.

Please send me a snapshot of yourself. Remember I haven't seen you for more than a year and one of the shooting party and those birds called "grouse", and in return I will remember to try & get you the red Arab shoes size 5 – (a nice small size) next time I am in Cairo.

I am glad to say the weather has at last begun to get a bit cooler, but we sadly want some rain to lay the dust. I don't think it has rained since March, & the whole countryside is a dustheap in consequence.

So glad to hear Gwynne has got a good job with a nice General. He'll be getting married next.

Kindest remembrances to you all and good wishes for the best of sport. Mind you shoot a Royal.

Yours v. sincerely
Reginald Hoare

⁓⊕ ⊕⁓

41. (20.10.17)

229th Inf Me
E.E.F. 20.X.17

Dear Violet,
It seems a long time since I last heard from you, but I dare say there is a letter now on its way out me, enclosing the latest snap-shot of yourself which I asked for. I hope by next mail to be able to send you the red leather shoes you asked me to get for you, as I have given the commission to an officer going on leave to Cairo to try & get me two pairs from the Arab bazaar, so that will be a pair for Monica too – if he is able to get them.

I shall be interested to hear something about this sport you had up at Cabrach & Glenfiddick & Clash: but I expect your father had some difficulty in getting guns.

I had a very good view of an air fight a few days ago. I was out with my men, & there were a few aeroplanes humming about, but we get so used to them we take very little notice. But suddenly one of them began firing, & I naturally thought it must be a Hun plane trying to machine gun us. I quickly looked up & saw it was an air fight and had the satisfaction of seeing our man polish off the Hun in about 4 minutes. It was very interesting to see the machines swooping and dodging just like two hawks. Our man shot the wings or planes off the Hun machine, but it did not "fall like a stone" at all but came down much more gradually than I expected. Nevertheless, the pilot was stone dead when we got to him.

That's the 2nd Hun plane we have bagged in the last week – Good business. Of course, they are not nearly so plentiful down here as they are in France, so we do not see many air fights; many may take place miles away out of sight.

Weather getting gradually cooler, but its plenty hot enough at mid-day.

I got v. wet with dew sleeping out on night operations last night (practise) but feel v. fit & well this morning in spite of only getting 4 hours sleep.

I hope you are all fit & going strong & will enjoy a good season's hunting.

Yrs v sincerely

Reginald Hoare

≈◎ ◎≈

42. (9/11/17)   229th Inf Bde
                                                                                              E.E.F.
                                                                                              Egypt
                                                                                            9.XI.17

Dear Violet,

Many thanks for your last splendid long letter which reached me on the Battlefield here (SHERIA) this morning.

We have been in the thick of it, & my Brigade bore the brunt of the attack on this place on 6th. We moved to a position of readiness for the attack at 11pm the night before, & waited till 4.45Am before commencing the advance; we then attacked over 5 miles of perfectly open bare country against Turks in deep trenches, but nothing could stop my fellows who were perfectly magnificent, & carried all before them, though the Turks put up a stubborn resistance and had to be bombed out of their trenches in some places. I had over 500 casualties in my Brigade but that is not very heavy considering the very open ground we had to attack over & the length of the advance. I had one Colonel killed & two other commanding officers wounded, but I am glad to say a lot of the wounded are "walking" cases.

I had one of my horses killed the day before.

We are now clearing up the battlefield, & refitting before our next move, but our Cavalry have pushed on a long way, and I hope are rounding up a lot more Turks as 52 prisoners came back through my bivouac last night. I think we've got the Turks on the run, and I hope it will be the end of them in this part of the world, though the campaign is far from being over.

My Divnl General came and wrung my hand the morning after the attack & congratulated me on the magnificent show put up by my Brigade. It gave me a horrid lump in my throat, as I felt that they had done it all themselves, & I had done so very little.

I've got a pair of your socks on now, & they are very comf, & a perfect fit.

No, I don't know any of those books you mention, & have little time for book reading, but do send one at a time. I am very fond of the "Long long trail".

Fancy you having to groom Pinkey. It's very dirty, dusty work. You ought not to do it, please. It's much too hard work for you.

I hope you have shaken off your bronchial cold. It must have been v. annoying getting it when you wanted to go out to a concert. I hope it was a great success.

Don't forget to send the snap shots of yourself — with hat — & without hat — <u>taken close up</u> so that I can recognise who it is ...

No more now.

Yrs v. sincerely

Reginald Hoare

43.(26.11.17)

229 Inf Bde On the March
26.XI.17

Dear Violet,

As letters from home are taking almost a month to reach me out here, this letter must take with it my Hearty Good wishes to you all for A Very Happy Christmas and lets hope that the war will be over before another Christmas comes round.

I am writing this on the March, and today have passed Askalon and Esdrid (Ashdod) and I was looking forward to seeing Joppa, but tomorrow we are going to turn more inland towards Jerusalem.

I hear it is a very mountainous and rough country in the hills round about that place, and we can see it from here. Some of the hills go up to 3,000 ft, & you can get snow up there. Today & yesterday we marched through an undulating plain, which looks very fertile & airy it would grow anything but being winter-time, the ground is bare of crops, & there is very little ploughing going on.

Gaza was in ruins, and a deserted city. I rode through the place some days ago and could not find a single house with the roof on. The Turks had demolished the lot, & removed all the doors, beams & rafters to build underground "dug outs" for themselves in their trenches, and we found them all there. It is also said that they wanted fuel for their railway engine.

They had even rescued a lot of paving tiles from the floor of the Mosque and other places to make paths to their hospital (Field Hospital), I suppose to minimise the dust and sand. But to tear up the floor of a Mosque is not the act of a true Mohammedan. They are very slack about their religion, and our Indian troops who are Mohammedans look down on them in consequence. They also used the big Mosque as an ammunition store.

I enclose as Xmas Cards a few photos for you which were taken shortly before these operations commenced.

We shall soon be up fighting with the Turks again, and I hope before long, you will hear that we have freed Jerusalem from the rule of the Young Turkish party, but we want to knock out the Turkish Army, and then we can go where we like. The country is getting more interesting and the population more numerous as we get further north; the inhabitants are very biblical in their appearance, & I am sure I saw both Moses & Aaron today, but the Jewish type of countenances is very common.

The Turks turned all the Jews out of Joppa a month ago, & treated them disgracefully – gave them no notice, and no means of getting their household goods away, but simply

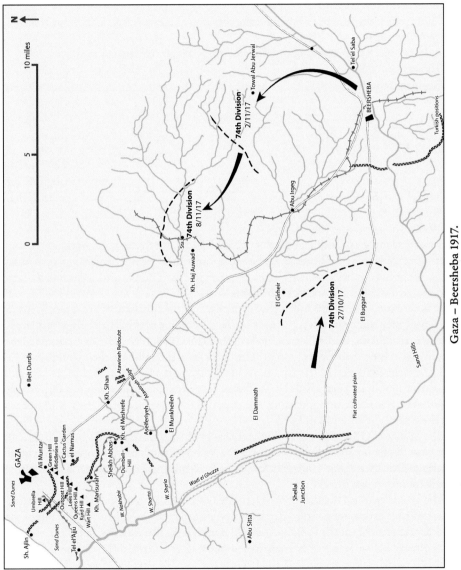

Gaza – Beersheba 1917.

cleared them out. However, we are now in Joppa, so I expect the Jews will come to us there for protection. We have been buying Jaffa (Joppa) oranges from Bedouin hawkers along the road during the march for the last 2 days, but most of them seem to me to be very unripe. They are quite green & I am very disappointed with them.

I expect the Bedouin have enjoyed some good sport hunting, but I don't suppose you have been able to do much of it.

I hear your father has been buying some yearlings at Newmarket, and I hope they will turn out all winners.

Jolly good luck to you, and best wishes for a very Happy Christmas to you all.
Yrs very sincerely
Reginald Hoare

❧ ☙

44. (18.12.17)

229" Inf Me
(near Jerusalem) E.E.F.
18.XII.17

Dear Violet,
Many thanks for your splendid long letter of Nov; 11 which arrived a good week before your father's letter of Oct: 31st. The mails are like that sometimes. Please thank him for his letter. Well, we've been & gone & done it. Jerusalem the Golden (I don't think), has fallen – and this days ago. I went & had a look at the town.

It is very interesting, but indescribably filthy, and the inhabitants are a motly crowd & look as if they came out of the Chorus in the Pantomine of Alibaba & the 40 thieves – English, French, American, German, Italian, Russian, Greek, Pole, Jew & Copt. religions are as mixed as the inhabitants (I forgot Americans) and they all have their churches.

I first went to the top of the American Hospital & got a fine view of the City, ancient & modern from there. Then I did the Garden of Gethsemane, & the mount of Olives. The Garden of G. is small & disappointing, but contains 6 old gnarled olive trees, said to have been there since the time of our Lord.

The Mount of Olives has v. few olive trees on it but several large modern buildings, but a fine view can be obtained from there over the Valley of the Jordan, & one can see quite a lot of the Dead Sea about 4000 ft below, & only 16 miles off. Very barren & uninviting looking country down there.

The attack by us on the defences of Jerusalem was well carried out. My Brigade had a very formidable task as they had to climb up a very steep rocky hill about 1500 ft out of the Valley & take trenches at the top. But they did it with only 12 casualties.

The night before was wet & cold, & the night after I slept in the captured Turkish trenches – v. cold – as we are about 2400 ft above the sea. The next night we had a hard frost with 1/4 in of ice on any buckets of water left out. Too cold to sleep – it was a very sudden change after the heat & dust we have lately been in, but we are getting used to it now, & it's a splendid air up here, & makes you as hungry as a hunter.

You must excuse my writing, but I have both hands bandaged up, as I have these tiresome septic sores which are so common out here. I think it must have been septic sores which Lazarus suffered from when "Moreover the dog came & licked his sores". Odd name for a dog – wasn't it?

I went & scrambled about these rocky hills yesterday after Hill partridges which are like the French Redlegged partridge at home, with the latch of Plarmigan as they live among the rocks. I enclose some feathers.

This is a rough country – fearfully steep hills, covered with stones & boulders, & with natural terraces of rock running round there – Very few roads, but we are making many more, & the old Roman roads are useless for traffic.

There is a village, or a tomb, or a ruin at the top of nearly every hill, & that makes a very odd landscape, as there are few trees about the villages.

We had nothing to do with the Capture of Gaza, as our Dismounted Yeomanry Divn attacked the other end of the line at Beersheba – over 30 miles from Gaza – but we marched all the way back there afterwards & started afresh from near Gaza for Jerusalem. I must try & get into Jerusalem again & buy you a few souvenirs, but there's not much there, I'm told. The Turks here cleared out nearly everything, but the City is quite undamaged.

I hope you are getting some hunting, & that Pinky is carrying you well. This is a rotten hunting country, though we saw a fox a few days ago, & there are just a few gazelles about. You couldn't possibly make a golf links up here either. It's all rocks & stones, & very rough on boots. Your socks are splendid, & very comfy and warm.

The Turks cleared out all the natives from any villages they wanted to live in themselves, but the inhabitants are gradually coming back again to them. The villages are indescribably filthy, and the houses are not recommended for human habitation as they are alive with insects.

Now I must stop this – Kind regards to you all & every good wish for 1918.
Yrs v. sincerely
Reginald Hoare[8]

───── ❦ ─────

45. (7.1.18)

229th Inf: Brigade
E.E.F.
7.1.18

Dear Violet,
Many thanks for your letter of Dec 17th & congratulations on having got to Jerusalem. We have been having strenuous times since then, and very wet, & uncomfortable times. On Xmas eve we rec'd order to march at once as it was reported that the Turks meant to attack & make an effort to retake Jerusalem.

We marched half through the night in pouring rain & arrived at our bivouac ground very wet, & nothing but very wet ground to bivouac on. Xmas day it <u>poured,</u> and on the following night we moved forward in preparation for delivering a counter-stroke at the Turks the following morning.

My Brigade had to creep down to the bottom of a steep rocky valley in the dark, & we

---

8   For a telling account of Brigadier-General Hoare's generalship during the subsequent 'Defence of Jerusalem' from Ottoman counter-attacks, see Appendix III.

hid till they got the order to climb up to the top of the hill opposite & attack the Turkish position at the top. The climb up took 1½ hours, though my General expected it to take 2 hours. (How long does it take to get to the top of the Buck?).

We had 3 days operations against the Turks and my Brigade did splendidly & were responsible for the capture of BEITAMIA — near RAM ALLAH the next day (28" Look at your map), as well as other commanding positions.

We captured 9 Machine Guns, took 135 prisoners including 6 officers, 2 of whom were Battalion Commanders, & the senior told us he had had orders to hold BEITAMIA to the last, but he did not know he was up against the "2 x 2 x 9". I buried 118 dead Turks the next day, & we collected over 300 rifles, so we gave them a rare hammering.

I got a personal letter of thanks afterwards from the Corps Commander [Lieutenant-General Sir P.D. Chetwode GOC XX Corps] but that does not mean that I was singled out for any special praise, as successes were general all along the line, and instead of the Turk retaking Jerusalem, he was driven back about 3 miles on a 10 mile front, and got a nasty smack in the eye into the bargain — losing a lot of men & M.Gs.

Your socks have been a great comfort to one this cold wet weather, & I've got a pair on now. It is very good of you sending me another pair — honestly that's enough.

I went into Jerusalem yesterday and attended the Intercession Service at the Cathedral. It was most impressive, and the mens voices "tugging away" at the well-known hymns sounded splendid.

We are now hard at work making roads so as to improve facilities for getting up supplies. This country is almost road-less, and lately we have had a breakdown on the railway, and the roads in such a wet and slimy state that even motor trollies could not get along, while the camels could not even start. So, we've had no Xmas parcels, & only a few letters – But nobody cares so long as we are winning the war. Food for man and beast must take first place, but the parcels will roll up before next Xmas.

So glad you enjoyed your trip to Ireland & got some sport. I used to hunt more in Meath then in Kildare when I was last there. I had two winters in Meath, and enjoyed capital sport, but I'd sooner hunt in England. I think hunting in strange countries is always v. interesting. I am so glad you were so well carried.

Cyclamens are out growing wild among the rocks, inspite of the cold & wet. We grow them under glass at home – Isn't it odd.

Kind regard & best wishes to you all.

Yours v. sincerely

Reginald Hoare

꧁ ꧂

46. (19.1.18)

Shepheard's Hotel
Cairo
Jan 19th

Dear Violet,

I have come down here, at my General's wish, for a few days change & rest, and it is very pleasant to sleep between sheets again, and to find oneself under a roof & enjoying a <u>real</u>

XX Corps GOC and attached formation commanders, L to R: Major-
General J.S.M. Shea (GOC 60th Division); Lieutenant-Colonel G.B. Watson
(CO 'Watson's Force'); Lieutenant-General Sir P.D. Chetwode (GOC XX
Corps), Major-General J.R. Longley (GOC 10th Division) and Major-General
E.S. Girdwood (GOC 74th Division), c. December 1917. (R. Hoare)

hot bath in a proper bathroom.

I yesterday went down to the "Muskji" or native part of the town and got you two
more pairs of slippers – You remember that this last lot I sent you I did not select myself, as
I was not in Cairo, but got a friend to get them for me, and I am afraid they were not very
satisfactory. I hope these are better, but they do not make them lined with lambswool. You
must get the lining put in at home.

Please examine the contents of the box carefully, as I have put in it a present each for
you & Monica, but you must have first choice. These presents I also bought in the native
bazaar, and one can get lovely things there.

Let me know how you like the things, and which you choose. I think I know which you
will choose – and if you like these kinds of things I can get more.

The Cairo Derby is run today, so I am off to the races to try and win enough money
to pay for the curious present of a Circassian worked cigarette case which I gave myself

yesterday – "To Reggie from Reggie".

I had a very rough journey down here & had to push the General's fore car many miles through boggy ploughed fields before we reached the nearest railway station – and it poured with rain most of the time – and when it rains up among the mountains of Judda it is "some downpour". My journey to the station took from 9.AM to 3.15pm – and the whole journey from my camp to Cairo took 25 hours.

I was taken to look in at an afternoon dance "for Lonely Officers" at the Continental Hotel near this hotel, yesterday. I believe Lady Allenby was instrumental in setting them up, and they are kept very select. I know none of the ladies, but was introduced to one or two, & sat out & looked on at the young 'uns enjoying themselves – I shall have to take dancing lessons when I come home, as the modern style of dancing the "Foxtrot" or whatever it's called is new to me, and then I shall be able to "trip it" with the best of them.

I left my Brigade hard at work making roads, & the General said they could make roads without me, and a few days change & rest would do me good – He is awfully pleased with my Brigade, & they have done splendidly – We made a big bag of prisoners & took 9 machine guns in the last "stunt" – last month.

I hope you are all very fit.

Kindest regards to you all.

Yrs v. sincerely

Reginald Hoare

⊰◦ ◦⊱

47. (27.2.18) Photograph <u>Enclosed</u>

229" Inf. Bde
E.E.P.
27.2.18.

Dear Violet,

It seems ages since I heard from you, but perhaps you have written, and your letter may have been sunk – Those Huns are so careless. I trust all is well with you. I enclose a photo of the "wise (?) men" of YALO, (the village where I am in bivouacked nearby). I had got them together to give them a lecture on Sanitation, with the aid of an interpreter, and a Doctor. The Village is indescribably filthy, and it's no wonder they get ill.

The head man, or "MUKTAR" of the Village, is in front squatting with his brother. We made these old "Grey beards" from the village run a race at some sports which we held a short time ago. Are they not biblical in their appearance? But they are dirty figs in their habits.

I started out today to make a long reconnaissance, but after an hour's ride, it came on to pour, so I "chucked it" and came back, as it was impossible to *see* any distance.

I am always most sorry for the men in wet weather in bivouac – especially if they have got wet, as they have no fires to get dry at, and all they can do is to "keep smiling", and "stick it out" till the sun shines again, when they spread all their things out to dry.

There are more wild flowers coming out now. In addition to the cyclamens, and bright scarlet ranunculus the size of poppies, like large anemones, there are small "Ragged Robins", and other little yellow & blue flowers, and some pinky-white lilies on long stalks. Would you like me to send you some bulbs?

I wonder if you have yet received the parcel sent off from Cairo, containing slippers etc.

I went out for a scramble over these rough, rocky hills with my General a few afternoons ago to try & get some partridges, but we saw very few till we had reached our boundary, & then they all went the wrong way. We only got a brace – saw a woodcock but did not get a shot at it – A fortnight ago we got 2 woodcock & a brace of partridges within 1/4 of a mile of my HdQuarters – Its very rough walking, & bad for one's boots.

The photo I send is of my own taking, as I have an "Ensign" camera now. (Could not get a Kodak) and I will send you a photo soon of "Reggie in 1918". When am I going to get the snapshots of yourself?

I hope you are getting some hunting & keeping fit.

Kindest regards to you all.

Yrs v. sincerely

Reginald Hoare

48. (9.3.18)

229" Inf Bde
E.E.F:
March 9th

Dear Violet,

Ever so many thanks for the box of "clothing", containing socks, soap – (nice Violet soap), book, and snapshots – It is awfully good of you to be such a fairy god-mother to me, and to send me such useful things. I cannot think why the parcel has been such a long time reaching me, as I got letters of Feb 12th a week ago, yet your letter is dated Dec 31st. Never mind – They have rolled up safely, but please send a letter separately in future & not in a parcel. Parcels are more likely to go astray & get "pinched" than letters. I think the snapshots are awfully good, and you look a dear in both of them – as you are, to send me such nice things, and to write so often.

We have finished one road making in the YALO district and have done a two days march forward, and our Division is now advancing the line and driving the Turks back still further. The attack on their positions commenced at dawn today, but as my Brigade was in the front line in the last operations, we are in reserve this time, and my men are hard at work day and night remaking the one and only road which runs Northwards in these parts.

I rode forward about 6 miles along it this morning as soon as I heard we had captured the first "objectives". The road is as bad as any farm track and The Turks have blown it up in several places & destroyed bridges & culverts. I was careful not to ride on the road when I got far in front, as we know that it has been mined in several places, and I did not want a "Voyage in the air" by being blown up.

I enclose the words of a song composed by one of my men and sung at our last open-air concert last Saturday. The poetry is shocking, and the rhyming bad, but it was a very popular song. When singing it, you must say "2-2-9", like "5.15", and I believe the other name for the song called "Casey Jones" is "the 5.15". It's a sort of rag-time or coon song.

You will have seen the account of our operations of today and tomorrow, long before this reaches you, in the papers.

I hope the concert went off well, and that you were in your best form with our farm"
and "Annie Laurie".

The country in front of us is still high rocky hills, with steep valleys in between. The
hills are terraced with rocks, and nearly every terrace is planted with Olive trees, Fig trees,
or Vines. The Olive trees are evergreen. The Fig trees at present have no leaves, but they are
just beginning to bud. The Vines are also bare of leaves – they are not trained in any way, but
just left to trail about as they grow on the ground.

Wild flowers are getting more plentiful, and some of the terraces are getting quite pink
with small "Ragged Robins". Cyclamens grow wild among the rocks, and there are also
small forget-me-nots, dwarf lemon coloured iris; bright scarlet anemones, and small purple
orchids. But give me England.

Write again & tell me all about your hunting. I hope you finish the season well & are
well carried by Pinkie.

Kindest regards to all at Ruckley, and again many thanks for the parcels and good wishes.
Yours very sincerely
Reginald Hoare

⚬⚬

49. (Easter Sunday.4.18)

229th Inf: Bde
E.E.F.
Easter <u>Sunday</u>

Dear Violet,
Many thanks for your splendid long letter of Feb 24", I am so glad to learn that the slippers
and their contents arrived safely and are liked.

I thought you would choose the blue slippers & lapislazuli: but what luck the amethyst
being Monica's birthstone. I did not know that when I sent it. Please let me know if there is
anything else I can send at any time, & I will do my best to get them for you – but you must
not mind having to wait. If Mon's slippers are too small, will she please send a piece of tape
giving the required length, & state colour preferred.

I think they make the slippers in Red, blue, green, and purple.

So, you prefer a waltz to any other dance – so do I – with a good partner, and on a good
floor with the waltz well played. I cannot understand these "Foxtrots". It doesn't seem to
me like dancing at all – merely promenading or jogging round the room anyhow – "any old
how" – I received my "bit of ribbon" a few days ago from HRH. the Duke of Connaught, as
he came to our part of the world, and presented medals & decorations to several officers &
men of our Corps. The ceremony went off very well, & the arrangements were perfect. We
had a guard of honour, a band, and a fine day for him which was lucky, as the weather has
been vile lately.

I though HRH was looking very well, but much older than when I last met him, which
was at dinner some years ago at St Dunstans (Lady Londesborough), now the Hospital for
Blinded Soldiers.

He was to have come to see the view to the front from a big hill TEL ASUR (look at your map) near my Bde Headquarters. (All right, Mr Censor. The Turks know we are there.) The hill is 3300 ft high, & commands a fine view, but it was found too difficult for him to get at – only rough rocky paths leading to it, so he was taken off by motor to another hill more easy of access.

Some of my lads brought off a topping raid a few nights ago (We are now in the front line) and brought back 45 prisoners – 4 of whom were officers including one Battn commander – They reckon they also "did in" about 25 Turks, & destroyed a Machine Gun, while my casualties were only 5 slightly wounded, so it was a good performance. I was warmly congratulated by one Corps & Divn Commander, but I had nothing to do with it, beyond supervising the arrangements.

The mud has been appalling lately – Horses, mules & men engaged in transport work bringing up supplies arrive daily plastered with mud from head to foot – I am so sorry for them – and then they have to stand in it all night – cold, wet, mud, & 3000 ft above the sea – Its pretty chilly for them, as of course there are no stables – But I built up high stone walls to give them protection from the wind, & they don't do so badly.

The wet weather is supposed to come to an end the last day of this month (March) – that is today. But it doesn't look like it.

I enclose a list of more questions for you to answer. Do you remember the other list beginning "What do you most admire in man, and woman?".

I hope you have finished this season well without any falls – Well done you. riding Longwater. I expect he gave you a splendid "feel". There is nothing like the feel of a good blood horse under one, they are so much more elastic & springy.

I am at present in command of the Divn as G.O.C. has gone to Cairo for a week, so I am living in his palatial marquee, but I don't find it so warm as a tent.

I hope you have had my letter thanking you for the socks, soap etc. – Nice Violet soap – and it was awfully good of you to think of sending it. If you do send shaving soap again, please send a stick of it, instead of a tablet – I always use shaving sticks.

I forgot to tell you that our Corps commander Kodaked me in the act of being decorated by H.R.H. and has promised to give me the negative.

I have been to church twice today (open air service), and one of the men had made a beautiful cross decorated with small white flowers for Easter. The wild flowers keep on increasing, & fresh varieties come in to bloom every week, but Cyclamens are still going strong, & have been out ever since January.

Now I must stop this. I hope you are all well at home & going strong. Let's hope that this big advance of the Huns will bring the War to a speedy & satisfactory end. I am confident Haig will be able to deal with them.

Yours very sincerely
Reginald Hoare

Wartime caricature of Brigadier-General Reginald Hoare. (Dudley-
Ward, *The 74th Yeomanry Division in Syria and France*)

Western Front 1918

50. (6.5.18)

At Sea
On the good ship "HUSH."
May 6th

Dear Violet,

The above address may surprise you – But I've not "got the sack" – yet. Nor am I coming
home sick – But "me and my little lot" are ordered to France and this will be posted when
we get there – Therefore please, when you are next writing address <u>B.E.F.</u> and not as before.

This is a fine boat, and there are other liners in the convoy carrying troops, and we have
both British and Japanese destroyers as escort. We have had fine weather & fairly smooth
water, and I have, as senior officer, a very good cabin, or suite of cabins with my own sitting
room, bathroom, & sleep in a big double bed, which is most luxurious.

We had a bit of excitement yesterday morning, as two "U-boats" were sighted, and our escort went for them; and they soon disappeared, & all was well.

I do not know what part of France we shall be sent to on our arrival. It depends upon how badly we are wanted. But I should think it unlikely that we shall be sent right up to the front at once. I expect we shall be given some special training behind the line first, and perhaps some of us may be given an opportunity of a run home. But it all depends upon the "military situation".

I liked the "Knave of Diamonds" very much, though I considered "the Knave" himself a horrid character, and I felt quite sorry that the charming lady who eventually married him was unable to find someone better.

I have known of our impending move for some time, but of course I could not say anything about it in a letter. Its rather nice to think one will be nearer home now – and I'm sure we are near the end of the war.

I don't know when you wrote last, but we have missed one or two mails in consequence of our move.

I hope you are all well at home, & going strong, & that "Invincible" will be "unbeatable" this season.

Yrs v. sincerely
Reginald Hoare

51. (19.5.18)

229th Inf Bd
B.E.F.
France May 19

Dear Violet,
Many thanks for your long letter of May 9th addressed to E.E.F., and also for one of May 11th – They both reached me here all right, as the Army Post, Office "switched them off", and put them on the right road – I'm afraid you'll get no Palestine bulbs or seeds from me now.

I am so sorry to hear Gwynne has had such a bad time with his face. It must have been horribly painful, glad to hear he is getting on all right now.

I don't know when I shall get any leave. Its nearly two years since I was last home, but I dare say we shall be given a run home before long, if we are not too busy "biffing the Boschs".

Lovely summer weather here the last few days, but we've all caught streaming colds from living in a house after living so long in this open air – Just like hunters out at grass in the summer they never catch a cold till you bring them in to stables in the autumn.

I met Sir Douglas Haig a few days ago looking v. fit & cheery, and we had a little talk about old times in the cavalry – I have also met other old friends out here whom I had not seen for a very long time.

It's a great treat too to get the London papers only a day old, instead of a month old.

Here are my answers to my questions:
1. Favourite colour – Light blue
2. Pastimes – <u>Summer</u> – Shooting & fishing, Tennis & Golf – Winter. Hunting

3. Favourite writer of <u>prose</u> – Haven't got one. I think it's a friend who will write to me
4. <u>Poetry;</u> Rudyard Kipling & Lindsay Gordon
5. Favourite song. God save the King. I am very fond of some of Henry Somersets – viz. Song of Sleep & Echo
6. Favourite flowers – Roses, Violets – Carnations

Now I think of some more conundrums for me.

In a way I am rather sorry to have left the other country we came from, as I should have like to have seen the end of the campaign out there; it was so very interesting. On the other hand it's nice to be nearer home in Europe once more, and after all this is the <u>main</u> show – the other was a "side show".

Kindest regards to you all,

Yrs v. sincerely

Reginald Hoare

<u>PS.</u> I see I have omitted to answer one of your questions, which was whether I had received a parcel & letter from you. Yes, I did, and I wrote you what I thought was rather a nice letter of thanks.

The parcel contained Soap – (nice Violet soap); socks (nicely made by Violet); and photos. I liked the photos awfully and I said so, & also said that you looked a dear in the photos, & you <u>were</u> a dear to be such a fairy godmother to me, & to send me such nice parcels – Did you never get that letter?

The socks are a perfect fit & so comfy, but I asked you not to send me any more for the present, as I now have plenty.

⁓❦ ❦⁓

52. (18.6.18)

229 Inf: Bde B.E.F.
18.6.18

Dear Violet,

Many thanks for your last letter, and I do hope you are quite strong and fit again and have had a good rest from your hospital work & nursing Gwynne.

You musn't go and overwork yourself, or you won't last out the war.

Your poppy border sounds lovely – There is no flower garden to this Chateau, but I went out two evenings ago & picked some ox-eye daisies & grasses out of the fields and decorated our dining room table with them.

We've had no rain here for a fortnight or more, and the crops want it, though the country is looking splendid.

Last Sunday I motored to the HdQtrs of a Division in the line to lunch with an old brother officer,[9] who commands it, & afterwards attended a Horse Show got up by the New Zealand Divn. I met a lot of old friends there and had quite a cheery afternoon.

Would you like to send me a book or two to read? If so I should be very grateful. I enjoyed the Knave of Diamonds but felt sorry for the charming lady who married the

---

9   Probably Maj. Gen. R.W.R. Barnes, late 4th QOH and member of the 1899 regimental polo team.

blackguard.

Its v. cold here, I find it, except <u>in</u> the sun, and we have had a fire the last two evenings, though I could have done without it. But as half the panes of glass are gone out of the windows of the chateau, a fire does not make the room very hot.

Do write & tell me how you are now. I hope you are quite fit and let me know when I am to have a bit on a family horse.

Yours very sincerely
Reggie H.

※ ※

53. (1.7.18)

B.E.F.
July 1st

Dear Violet,
Ever so many thanks for the 3 books which arrived safely yesterday, it is very good of you to have taken the trouble to send them.

Unfortunately, I have read two of them "The Way of an Eagle", and "Candle in the Wind", but they will bear reading again.

I personally get little time for reading, except about 20 minutes in bed just to send me to sleep. But somebody is always in want of a book.

I am so glad you feel better for your change & visit to your aunts, but I am much concerned that you "don't feel a bit yourself and can do very little without getting so tired". I shall have to come home and prescribe for you. I hope that with summer come at last, the warmer weather will do you good.

I was awfully pleased to see Artsman's win in the paper, but I have not had a bet for two years, as we know nothing about any racing till after the races are run, and then we see the accounts in the papers.

There were some very nice horses, officers' chargers etc. at the horse show, and one beautiful blood horse in particular caught my *eye,* which I was told had carried Freeman, the Pytchley huntsman, for two seasons.

There was a jumping competition too, but I could not wait to see that.

I hope the "perfect hack & hunter" which you are going to see will turn out to be what you want.

It is odd your mentioning oxeye daisies & grasses as making a pretty table decoration, as only a few days ago I went into the fields and picked them for our table & did the decorations myself.

We have moved since I last wrote, and the last success which was in the papers 2 days ago (when 401 prisoners & 22 Machine guns were taken) took place not far from where I now am.

I am now in a very nice chateau, smaller than the last one, but in a much better state of repair – glass in all the windows. It stands in its own little park away from the main road, so we are free from the dust and noise of motor trollies, but we are more bothered by the noise of guns, and have been kept awake the last two nights by the Bosch flying over after dark & dropping bombs which make the house shake, & one cannot get to sleep till after he has finished his duty work & gone away again.

A niece of mine who is a "Unit administrator" in the WAAC's out here, had a very rough time of it last month.[10] She was at Calais with 200–300 girls under her, but their camp got destroyed by the "Flying Fritz" dropping bombs at night so she was moved to Abbeville, and that place got visited by the Bosch night after night. One bomb dropped 1 1/2 yards from where she was and the poor WAAC's had had several casualties, altogether from these successive Air-raids, I believe it was about 6 killed & 15 wounded. And my niece was finally sent home to get some sleep.

However, she is none the worse, and expects soon to be out here again. She has been "mentioned in despatches", and her younger sister has had a Red Cross Medal as she has been working in a hospital ever since the War started. They are both awfully "bucked" about it.

Please thank your father for his letter. I must write an answer to it presently.

I hope when next you write you will be able to give a better account of yourself.

Again, many thanks for the books.

Yours very sincerely

Reginald Hoare

<hr />

54. (21.7.18)

B. E. F.
July 21st

Dear Violet,

Many thanks for your letter of 19th, just received – I am so glad to hear that you are "ever so much better", and I dare say the good war news, and the good racing news combined has helped to bring about a rapid recovery, which I hope will be permanent.

My name has been sent in for a Senior officers' course of instruction in Machine Guns at Grantham from Aug 5th to 8th, and I am asking for 3 weeks leave after the course at Grantham is over, but I do not know whether my name will be accepted for the Grantham course, nor whether my leave will be granted. A good deal depends upon what this Bosch is doing.

I was very pleased to see your father's two wins at Newmarket, and I hope he will gain many more successes before the season is over. Invincible must do something yet to justify his possession of such an ambitious name.

The success of the French counter-attack is really wonderful, and it is most cheering. It will be bitterly disappointing, and demoralising to the Bosch, as of course their plans are now quite upset by their being "biffed" back again. In the meantime, British operations north of here resulted in over 450 prisoners being taken, as well as 44 Machine Guns and 10 French Mortars, so that's not a bad little parcel.

I will let you know if I do get home Aug 5th – 8th, in case you should be in London about then, then we must do a play together – I've not seen a play for over two years. And I simply shall not know myself in a "boiled" shirt & Evening dress clothes.

Quite cool today, after some heavy rain yesterday when I got wet through walking

<hr />

10   I can only assume this was one of two (Emma and Grace) children of RH's sisters.

round the trenches.

We had two very hot & sultry days at the beginning of the week, which ended in thunderstorms.

Very busy so must stop this. Please congratulate your father on his wins, and with kind regards to you all,

Yours very sincerely
Reginald Hoare

55. (20.8.18)

Aug 20th
4.15 pm.

See if you can "spot" anything in this letter.

My Darling,

The train has just started, & I saw the last of you pluckily waving you hand at the back of the station till I was out of sight. It was very sweet, & very brave of you to insist on seeing the last of me, & you bore up (Beloved I love you darling) splendidly like the brave little woman that you are. And now that the parting is over – though its only for a time – I've got such a lump in my throat as I write, & Im rather "snuffily" inclined – I try & console myself by saying its tears of joy which want to come out, due to my great good luck in have won the love of such a darling as you are, and it still seems almost too good to be true. I wonder if you will "spot" anything in this letter, which will be continued later.

Aberdeen – 5.40 pm – No niece to meet me. I dare say she never got my letter, so I shall finish this & post it here, in order that you will get a letter from me sooner than you expected. Good news in the paper – our troops are now in MERVILLE & have taken over 600 prisoners – That is partly your Reggie's Divn (The 74th Divn). They are now east of the Paradis – Merville Road.

Just one question before closing. Have you changed your mind yet?

God bless you always little sweetheart & keep you safe till I come back.

Always Your devoted Reggie[11]

---

11   RH must have been on a course and obtained some leave to Scotland for some grouse at Cabrach before proposing marriage on 18 August 1918. Maybe the spot was a tear stain?

56. (21.8.18)

Telephone Nos. (6955/6956) Mayfair
Fleming's Hotel,
9&10, Half Moon Street,
41 & 42, Clarges Street,
Mayfair, W.1.
21st.
5.pm
Telegrams,
Grammateus, May,
London

Dearest Little Darling in the whole world – I've finished all my shopping for you, & I hope you will like the things I have sent – If you don't like the ring, <u>mind</u> you say so. Of course, I saw many nicer ones after I had bought that & I was rather taken with an emerald set in a square of diamonds, only it would have been too broad for your dear little finger. You told me not to get a broad ring.

Make Mother give you one of the bottles of solidified Eau de Cologne – you'll find it handy to carry, & v. refreshing to put on your temples, or behind your ears at any time when you are feeling a bit tired & headachy. It's also good to put on a midge bite – (when your Reggie isn't there to "Kiss the place & make it well!).

I hope you got back safely & slept well. I had quite a good night in the train. Finished off my dentist, who was very pleased with the state of my "dining room furniture". Had my hair cut. Lunched with an old friend who works at Devonshire House – a Miss Williams, niece of Gen: Sir Albert Williams – You need not be jealous she is much older than you & getting very grey, but a good cheery soul. My brother Bertie is coming up from Aldershot to dine with me at the Berkeley, & I have got 2 stalls for the Gaiety afterwards – <u>How</u> I wish it was going to be you instead. Now I must set to work & get packed up, & get rid of my shooting things etc.

This is quite a comfy hotel to stay, small & old fashioned – <u>We</u> must stay here some time. It's nice & quiet. My train goes at 8 AM tomorrow, & I breakfast on the train.

No more now, & please ask your mother to excuse my writing to her the usual guest's letter for the present, I am rather rushed for time, and can only find time to write to my darling. I will write again from Calais.

I hope you will like the songs. The words of two of them are very appropriate.

God be with you, and Keep you safe from all harm – Bless you, <u>bless</u> you, bless you
Your devoted
Reggie

57. (22.8.18)

HOW I wish I was at
Cabrach Lodge,
Rhynie,
Aberdeenshire.

P.S. You won't get the photos for 10 days or a fortnight.

Dover
11am 22nd

Dearest and best Beloved, here's a bit of luck for you. You'll get an extra letter from me, as on arrival here by the special leave train, we are told the boat will not sail till 3 pm, so I have come to a little clean "pub" to rest & write to you. You will also get another letter from me which I shall post at Calais, (by order of my darling).

I found it Very hot & stuffy in London, & I could not face the photographer again. I hope you don't mind. Bariano will send you up 2 of each which you have selected. But I could not order any frames till I know which size (or sizes) you liked best. If you want one painted up, they have noted the colour of my eyes (do you know their colour yet? You've looked into them often enough, you darling little Brown mouse.) But you must now send the order to them to do what you want with the photos. They will be much improved when "finished". But I don't think I shall be improved by "painting" though the colours of the medal ribbons, & red & gold gorget patches" will show up more.

I've got your photos in front of me as I write & have just kissed them & also the dear little "hankie".

By the bye, there is an oil painting of me in Hussar uniform by Mark Milbanke. Would you like that at Ruckley – to be later moved to our nest, or rabbit-hutch – when we find one. It's a dreadful portrait taken soon after the S. African war, when I was neither so old, so bold, or so bald, as I am now – (So bold to have dared to ask you to marry me.) and you'll have to hang it at the far far end of a big room, or entrance hall or long passage – It's too frightful to be seen close. If your father & mother or you would like it at Ruckley, I will tell my sister Ivy to send it there by what date? And I shall not be offended if you think it's too frightful, & you refuse to hang it on any wall.

I have told my two favourite sisters to write to you. They are Katie Gough, & my youngest sister Ivy – 2 years younger than myself, and she is the youngest of our family of "Methuselahs" – and I enclose a whole list of the family, half of whom you will never meet probably.

I meant to have sent you some hatpins, to "make good" the one who lost his head on Sunday Aug 18th. By the bye the 18th is a very propitious date for me & you. I was born on Sept 18th, 1865. We got engaged on Aug 18", and if it's a suitable date we might be married on ___18" – if we cannot be married on ___1st.

I want you to write me a very nice letter to reach me on Sept 18", my birthday, & I'd love to have the locket that day, if you could manage it – and please could you get into one side of the locket just the tiniest little sprig of white heather to bring me luck.

I hope you'll like some of the songs. Do get also Henry Somerset's "Song of Sleep". I'd like you to learn that, but you must not depress yourself by singing nothing but sentimental sort of songs. I'd like my darling to learn a bright cheerful song or two too. How I shall look forward to hearing your voice again. Why are you here at this minute. How I wish you were.

Violet photographed during Brigadier-General Hoare's home leave.

If the ring is too large it can be made smaller. If too small it can be made larger. I actually was a Very little bigger than your size given me by you.

I am now going to touch on a delicate subject – I cannot help thinking that all the cooking at the V.A.D. hospital which my darling has been doing, has not done her complexion any good. I would not have you with a white complexion or pasty faced for worlds. I just love your sweet face. But have you ever tried Beecham's Lait Larola. It is most cooling, & soothing, & would be just the thing to put on after cooking or when your cheeks are burning, or before going out of doors, or when you come in again. Your Reggie uses it on his funny old mug after shaving sometimes, or in the winter when there's a cold wind, & the washing water is hard. You can buy it at almost any Chemist for 1/- a bottle, & I feel sure you could get it at Huntly or Aberdeen. I swear by it, or perhaps it would not suit your skin. Anyhow will you try it, & also forgive me for alluding to such a delicate subject.

I hope you are sleeping well & have not lost your appetite – when writing will you please report on your state of health, appetite, and "sleepitite". Your "drink-itite" does not worry me so much. But as a good change from "Adam's ale", try Dry Ginger ale with a slice of lemon in it. The ginger is good for one, & the slice of lemon in it takes off the sting of the ginger & makes it more refreshing.

I dined with my brother Bertie (Herbert his name is really) at the Berkeley last night. It was hot and crowded, & attendance bad, then we went to the Gaiety, but I did not enjoy it a bit – because you were not there with me. I thought it a silly rotten play, & could not find a good tune, or good song in it.

I did not sleep well last night, I was thinking a lot about you, & wondered if you were sleeping all right. God send you sweet refreshing sleep always, my darling. I lay awake till 2 or 3, & then had to be called at 6, to catch the 8 o'clock leave train – only to arrive here at 10.30 to be told the boat does not go till 3pm. Please also try the Larola on your chest & neck. (I hope you don't mind my suggesting this) but personally I, with many other men do not admire a scorched neck & chest. A sunburnt face is quite another thing – but I can see nothing to admire in a scorched chest; that <u>ought</u> to be whiter. I think. But if the fashion for ladies to wear low necked dresses in the daytime, & so they get their neck scorched.

I suppose the blouse with collar & tie is out of date, otherwise I would suggest you having that hanky I gave you made into a tie to tie in a sailor's knot.

And now little sweetheart (I have not called you that before – Do you like it or not?) I have a very senior question to ask you, so sit back, & hold tight. No, you need not shut your eyes. Just look me straight in the face, and answer this – "Have you changed your mind?" (What a shame to tease my Darling like that. But she will find me an awful tease), I should like your reply to that question to be three _____ which stand for three simple words viz "*I love you*, and therefore I have NOT changed my mind.

Let me know always if there is anything in any-of my letters which you don't like or don't understand – which do you prefer? or do you dislike any of these – "Sweetheart", "Best beloved", "My little Brown Mouse", "Brownie". Personally, I prefer you calling me "Old <u>Boy</u>" to "old <u>man</u>" – Let's be boy & girl as long as we can, see? Write me fully, freely, all your thoughts. If you write me a stiff formal cold letter, I shall think you have changed your mind. We are going to be "pals", real pals, comrades, chums, & play fellows, as well as lovers.

Now I must stop & get some lunch. I've been writing to you for 2 hours. How I wish you were here. I don't think I should want any lunch then.

God bless you my dearest darling. You have all my love; and God grant that I shall prove worthy of yours.

Your devoted Reggie.

Love to Mon & your mother

P.S.
You want to send me something – send me some lavender bags to put among my undies". And I want a little 2-fold frame to stand your photos up in – please.

⁓⊙ ⊙⁓

58. (24.8.18/26.8.18)

B.E.F.
24"
6pm

My darling,
I have been out all day, and on my return, I find your dear letter – the first from you since the great and wonderful event of our engagement, and of our parting. Thank you so much for it, and bless you for missing me so, and for all the dear, nice things you say in your letter. I haven't time for much of a letter as I expect my staff officers in every minute with a lot of papers to sign. Here he is.

I went for a long walk yesterday & today over the ground we have lately won back from the Bosch between Merville & L'Epinette. The devastation is dreadful to look at, and the ground is pitted with shell holes every few yards.

In some place where there is a church marked on the map, I could not find the Church, as next to nothing is left of it, but I realised I was on the site of the Church because of the graveyard & tombstones alongside of the ruins.

I picked up 3 Bosch steel helmets which I am sending to your father. They are the only souvenirs we are allowed to send home. Please ask him to let you keep one at least for our home. How do you like the sound of our home? It appeals to me very much. I dined with my G.O.C. Divn last night, & told him of my engagement, He was charming to me, & begged for your address so that he might write & congratulate you. I hope he won't pile it on too thick, as I feel sure he is inclined to grossly exaggerate any good qualities he thinks I may possess. I met our Corps Commander at dinner, & he was in great form, and very pleased with our Divn.

By the bye, the best map for you to get is Stanfords ½inch map of the British front in France and Flanders, No. 23. I think its No. 23. & Stanfords Ltd 12 Long Acre – London W.C. is the address, but any good Bookseller in Aberdeen or Edinburgh should have it. It's about 14/– or 15/–, I have slept very well since I got out here, & I hope you are sleeping well too. Let me know, won't you, dear.

Don't let Gwynne practise with his rifle on my Bosch helmets. I feel sure he'd like to do so.

I saw the announcement of our engagement in the "Times", & "Morning Post", and was very pleased to see it.

I do so wonder when the happy day will be when I shall really call you mine, MY Violet. God for ever bless you & Keep you safe from all harm – my dearest darling.

Your loving & devoted Reggie.

This will be posted in London by an officer coming home on leave, who will also send off the Bosch helmets. I hope you will get the letter all the quicker.

⚮

59. (24.8.18/26.8.18)

B.E.F.
26"

My own darling,

Yes, you are a darling and my darling. Again, many thanks for your letter of 22nd Which reached me today (this will not be posted till tomorrow). Such a nice letter you wrote me, and I am so pleased to learn that you slept so well in my room. How I wish I had been there to fondle & caress you – but thats a bit premature.

I love your saying "October will not be too soon"- I spotted it and I wish it was going to be earlier than that. I'd just love you to put your arms round my neck and take away a lumpy feeling in my throat. Our love for each other seems to have grown since our parting. I am yearning to see you again, but I've got my duty to do out here, and I must devote myself to that, much as I should love to devote myself to you only. I have had lots of letters of congratulations and I expect you'll hear from some of my family too. The book of the "in-laws" may amuse you. Lots of them are grandfathers, & grandmothers, & I'm a great-uncle.

I have asked my General to be my best man. He is a Widower – lost his wife during the war, but he's a good many years younger than I am – I don't know whether he'll be able to manage it, & I don't think I can send one of his photos on approval. But I'm sure the Bridesmaids will find him kiss-able.

I've been biking & walking about the country near Merville. The Bosch was shelling Merville so "I gave it a miss", but I had to put on my gas mask, or box respirator, in one place where the brute had been putting down some gas-shells. But I only wore it for a few hundred yards & took it off as soon as I had got out of the gassed area. I hope the cold is not going to be a bad one. I wish I could come and Kiss it away. I was thinking of you nearly all the afternoon, & was out from 2 to 6.30 pm, & got wet through, as it came on to rain quite hard on the way back.

I enclose an advertisement about "Larola". I hope you don't mind my giving you the suggestion. Perhaps you know the stuff quite well. Your Reggie uses it sometimes, which accounts for his "blooming cheek" (or beautiful? complexion).

I slept well last night but was wakened up once or twice by a few shells which dropped somewhere in our neighbourhood, but I soon dropped off to sleep again. God send you sweet refreshing sleep always, my darling – for I only know that I want you so, and no one else will do. Are you yearning for your Reggie, as much as he is yearning for you? If so, it's a pretty big "Yearn". You will find great difficulty in getting anything done in the way of clothes in London or anywhere else. They simply take ages to do anything now – but I don't mind if you are married in a walking dress, so long as I've got you.

God bless you & Keep you safe my darling. Always your loving and devoted Reggie. Please give any of my love which you can share to the family.

⚜

60. (25.8.18)

B.E.F.
25"

Dearest Darling,

Many thanks for your second letter written on 21st which reached me here this morning. And so you liked my first letter very much & it gave you a big lump in your throat. Bless you for feeling like that. If you only knew how full my heart has been at leaving you, and how very "gulpy" I have felt too. But now I have other things to think about; and am very busy. But you are seldom out of my thoughts for long, and I find myself wondering what you are doing at this minute several times during the day.

And so, my best beloved has been & gone & caught a cold. Poor darling, I am so sorry – I hope it won't be a bad one, & that you will soon shake it off – You must tell me in every letter how it is. I loved your missing me so out shooting and find the butts so cheerless without your Reggie to Welcome you into his. Yes darling. I spotted something in the letter – Bless you for wanting me so, & for saying you love me so. I am a lucky man to have gained the love of such a darling little brown mouse, and I hope I shall be able to make a very comfy 'nest' for my little brown mouse, & that she will be very happy in it.

You musn't mind if there are intervals between my letters, but I don't think you have much to complain about yet. What reams I have written you, darling, but I have loved writing to you – cos Why? Cos I love you – and I believe I've loved you for quite a long time, only you didn't know it, and I barely realised how much I cared for you. It was this day week, the "great" question was put to you, and I saw the lovelight shining in your dear eyes, and it seemed to increase daily since that date. How I wish I could see you now (7.30pm).

I've not been to any church today because there was no service near & I have been very busy.

Now I must "dress for dinner" – Which frequently means only taking off my spurs & having a bit of a wash. I shall not forget to drink your health, and when I drink my darling's health I say to myself "God bless you my darling, darling Violet".

I don't think I have sent any nice messages to any of your family, but my thoughts have been all for you, & for you only.

Please give my love to your mother & Mon. What bricks they both are. But my best love, and all my real love is for you, you dearest little Darling in the whole world.

Always your loving & devoted
Reggie

⁓◉ ◉⁓

61. (27.8.18)

B.E.F.
27"

My own dearest Darling,
So glad to get your letter of 23rd telling me the ring has arrived & that you like it. I am afraid I am horribly jealous of that ring, being so close to you, while I'm so far away. I was afraid it might be too big, but the other one I like was bigger still, & I wanted you to get a ring from your Reggie quickly. Darling, it's not nearly good enough for you – and the next ring I give you will be a better one than that. Let me know what you'd like it to be.

So glad you like the Lily of the Valley scent I sent – I didn't know whether you'd like it or not, and if you find after all you prefer Penhallfins I shan't mind. I am so glad that is your favourite scent – I don't know anybody else that uses it, & I don't want anybody else to use it – I don't think I ever smelt it before, & I like it at once. It is a nice light clean fresh smell – I dislike a heavy clinging sort of scent, don't you?

I laughed at myself sending you soap, as if you were not a nice clean sort of darling already. I wish I was near enough to be thanked by you – How would you thank me? Would you put your arms round my neck and kiss me very lovingly?

It's perfectly splendid your pretending to be jealous of Miss Williams – Will you believe me when I tell you that you are the only girl I have ever kissed, & the only girl I have ever asked to marry me. We are not a kissing family: but I found myself letting myself go a bit with you, didn't I. I am sure you still owe me some of the 64 I won off you by straight shooting at the grouse. What a ripping day that was. I was so happy with you. Dear little pal. Bless you for being anxious about me, & wishing I had wired you – I cannot wire from France – All wires are reserved for official military use – If I wanted to wire you, the wire would go by post to Folkestone or Dover, & then be wired from there: so they take about 24 hours to get anywhere, & by that time a letter would almost reach the same destination. Therefore, if I came home in a hurry, I should get home almost as soon as the wire.

So sorry you had to spend most of 23rd in bed – I wish I had been there to come & see you, & to kiss you to make you well. I hope you are up and about & frisking your tail again now, my darling little brown mouse – and I am glad to learn the cold is better.

I can't understand it. You say you have not changed your mind YET. It's very odd. But neither have I, & I shall not change my mind until we have the most awful row, & you tell me that you have changed. And then I shall put my arms round you and kiss you & tell you that you have not; and if you dare to say you have, I'll stop your mouth with kisses. Would you like that? I love your mouth.

If you want a good London bootmaker Faulkner – 51 South Molton St Bond St is my bootmaker, with Ladies dept. He is A.1 but it takes a long time to get anything done now.

If you want a good dentist, Warwick James, 2 Park Crescent, is very good. I'd like my Violet to take care of her teeth. I go to a dentist once or twice a year whether there is anything wrong or not. My dentist is George Hern – 7 Stratford Place. Very good & quick, but he was away for his holiday when I got home so I went to Warwick James instead, & I'm not sure I didn't like him better than my own man.

What else can I write about. Oh. The weather of course. We've had some heavy thundershowers, & the country was very muddy & sticky this morning. I took my lunch out with me, & rode, biked, & walked during my rounds.

Please Violet, I feel rather guilty that I never gave the driver (of the car of Watts which took us down to Huntly) any tip. Will you give him something from me, & I'll repay you in Kisses or coin which ever you prefer. If its coin, I'll throw in just a few kisses as well – so you'd better choose 'coin' then you'll get both – Sly girl.

Will you think out & let me know if there is any kind of jewellery, ring, brooch, necklace or bangle which you'd like your Reggie to give you? I want your Reggie always to give you something which you want particularly – I mean, I don't want to give you a thing, & then to find you'd sooner have had something else; or that you don't like the style or colour of the thing I'd given you. So, will you think of something, the next thing for me to give my Darling.

28th Slept so well last night, & I hope you did too. I hope the cold will be gone before this reaches you.

I dare say some of the "in-laws" will ask you to stay with them when you cone South. Mind & let me know your address at Harrogate & elsewhere ages before you go, or my letters won't reach you in time to catch you. If, I get another letter from you today, I'll write again. I hope the Bathe will do your mother good.

Bless you dearest darling
Your loving & devoted
Reggie

᠆ᘏ ᘜᣟ᠇

62. (29.8.18)

B.E.F.
29"

Dearest Darling,
Here is a letter for you begun in the train, as we are being moved to another part of France.

We have done good work where we were, and now we shall be put into Reserve until we are wanted again. I got no letter from you yesterday, but I am not complaining. You have been awfully good about writing, and I'd far sooner you only wrote to me <u>when you are in</u> the mood for it – Then I know I should get a genuine nice letter, instead of a letter which was perhaps rather forced. But I am sure you will be pleased to hear that I <u>missed</u> your letter. "Cos" why? "Cos" I love getting letters from my Darling – (capital D please for Darling – <u>my</u> Darling.) I think too that we should aim at a perfect understanding of each other, don't you dear? That is, I shall understand why you have not written & not worry about it, while you too will understand if you do not hear from me & <u>you</u> won't worry either, at present I think I have written to you every day, though I don't know whether you have got my letters daily – I wonder if you find your Reggie difficult to understand. Do you darling? I know I make friends – what I call <u>friends</u> & not merely acquaintances – slowly, and am reserved & rather shy, and difficult to get to know – Do you think you have got to know me? I want you to <u>know</u> me, and for us to have a <u>perfect understanding</u> of each other, and mutual sympathy. It <u>must</u> make for one happiness. I know my Darling is in love with me and wants me, and I know I am in love with her and want her. I know too that I found our evening together in the Drawing room, and our drive down to the station with my arms round you very – what shall I call it – "intoxicating". I was just yearning to make you mine, and my Darling seemed so responsive, and that made me love her so. I felt we were very near each other during that drive down to the Station – It was <u>delicious</u> and would have been <u>heavenly</u> if only we had been driving away on our honey-moon instead of being just about to part. Will you write & tell me, little sweetheart, just all <u>you</u> felt & thought at that time. Do write me your thoughts & feelings. I'd love you to it is thus that we shall arrive at a <u>perfect</u> understanding of each other – My Darling, <u>HOW</u> I love you, and HOW I want you. For I love you so, & I want you so and no one else will do. You have simply got me yearning, & forever I'll be true; let the great big world go on turning round, now I love a darling little brown mouse who loves me, and we both want each other, and we are so happy in our love for each other, and we are going to be such pals, playmates, comrades, & companions. Isn't all that true? Don't you think we are well suited for each other? I do – We have so much in common, and I think we are going to be <u>awfully</u> happy together. And my little Darling has become <u>very</u> dear to me, and <u>so</u> precious. I shall take <u>such</u> care of her, and cherish her, & very likely spoil her if I find she is <u>very</u> fond of me. I could not spoil anyone who did not care for me. Its <u>knowing</u> that you care for me makes me want to give you everything & to spoil you. Bless you Darling. You have promised to love, honour & obey your Reggie – Very well then – Come here. Put your arms – your loving arms – round my neck and Kiss me <u>lovingly</u> and I'll repay your Kisses a hundred-fold.

I say Vi. Do you like this kind of a letter, or would you rather I did not write this kind of drivel? Perhaps it gives you rather an attack of the "dithers" as you call it – Perhaps you don't call it drivel – It's just my thoughts that I have written to you – as if you were here talking to me. I suppose it's what would be called a "love letter" – Now I'll write in a more ordinary way.

We left our last place 2 days ago, that is I was relieved in the front line, and I had to sit up till 3 A.M. till the relief was completed – then we marched back to billets. Last night we entrained at 11.30pm & were told the journey would only take 7 hours but it's now 10.45 AM & we've some way to go yet. It's only a troop train – men in trucks, & I am only in a 2nd Class compartment, but I've just got some hot water from the engine and had a good shave

& a wash, & brushed my teeth, & I dare say my Violet would not mind Kissing me now, as I am nice & clean. I love the feeling of being clean, & I like nice clean looking, tidy people.

Please Vi are you hunting about among the advertisements for a house for us to live in, because we are going to be married, aren't we?

I enclose some I discovered yesterday, but I must leave you to do all the house hunting, & you must get Mon to help you.

I have however discovered that wives may come out here. One of my officers has got his wife in Paris already, and another has his in Trouville – That's a great place for bathing in the summer Trouville – I believe it's a charming place – much smaller than Nice – but very fashionable in the Yachting & bathing season. What would my Violet like to do? The idea of marrying you & leaving you behind when I return to France is horrid – But at the same time we must have a house to live in at home, & now is the time to start looking about for one – I'll get my sister Ivy to help you – She is very practical, & level headed. We could take a furnished house & see if we like the neighbourhood. Any neighbourhood you like but we should like some hunting, shooting & fishing if we could get it. Not too suburban a place, but I don't know whether my Darling would like to live right away in the country in too wild a spot. I think Dorset or Somerset might be tried – Devon is lovely.

Now I must stop this. Please look out in "Country Life" & other papers for a likely house. I suppose we shall want 6-8 bedrooms really then someone can come stay with us. I have no objection to Yorkshire, Shropshire, North going as far south as Hampshire – Wiltshire, Dorset or Devon – Where would my Darling like to live? We need not settle all over but could try one or two places.

I don't think it would be quite wise for you to come to Paris or Trouville except for a short visit When I could get leave to come to you. One can get 7 days leave in France more easily than one can get 14 days leave at home.

All my love & kisses. Bless you always.

Your devoted Reggie

⚜

63. (30.8.18)

B.E.F.
30"

My Darling,

No less than 3 letters from you arrived today. Ever so many thanks for them – All such nice letters too. I am so glad my darling was not offended at my mentioning the delicate subject of the complexion. I want you to know dear that I'd far sooner you were burnt as brown as a berry, than went in for a carefully preserved "touched up" London complexion. So, don't let the complexion question worry you anymore.

In addition to your 3 letters I had something like 20 others, mostly letters of congratulation from relations & friends, but several requests from firms asking for photos, order for flowers for our wedding & addressed "c/o Miss V. W." The address made me laugh "care of". I wish I was in your care at this moment. But I shall be one of these days. Will you take care of your Reggie, as well as care for him? I know you will.

Certainly, accept the offer of being photoed for nothing when you are in town, and I

RAMC stretchers-bearers of 12th Somerset Light Infantry, 229th Brigade, 74th Division, August 1918. Note the attached American medical officer seated in centre. (Private collection)

hope you will come out with a "broad grin" on your face. That's the way I like you best – looking happy in your love for me, and confidently happy in my love for you – Bless you for saying you miss me more every day – By the time you get this you will be able to say "I'm going to be married to my Reggie <u>next month</u>" (perhaps). I am sorry to have to put in "perhaps", but of course it all depends upon the Bosch, but everything is going splendidly so far. I want you to realise that I must leave all the details of the wedding, & honeymoon to you & your family. I don't mind <u>where</u> we are married, and if Ruckley is most suitable, make it so.

I am sure you will find my sister Ivy most helpful in any way, if you can only get her away from her V.A.D. work, which is not easy, as she can only get holidays now & again. She has got a good head on her shoulders, & I'm sure you'll love her.

I suggest your waiting till you get my photos from Bassano, before deciding which one to have coloured – You may not like any of them – I have told them to send you some of each to choose from yourself, & then to distribute them to your family or keep as you like – Some are also being sent to my family.

About the oil painting of myself – I am sure you will find it too big to hang in any small room but do what you like with it. I know Ivy won't mind sending it to you – in fact she reminded me of its existence in case you cared to have it. Its a horrid thing really, & only bears looking at <u>from a distance.</u>

I slept like a top last night, but I made no attempt to "put that tiresome girl" out of my head. Please you are <u>not</u> to call yourself that. You are my dearest Darling, & <u>the</u> dearest Darling in the whole world to me. I found myself whistling "and when I tell them, how wonderful you are" this morning, & thinking so of you. I felt so fit & well & young.

I had a most delightful ride over this new country which we are now in & wished you had been riding with me.

So, you like being called "Sweetheart". I feel I want to call you that when you are in my arms – when I am feeling <u>Very</u> much in love – a sort of <u>special</u> expression of endearment – not to be made too common – I love to think I may be wearing a chain which has been round my Darling's neck. Do you know the words of the second verse of "Drink to me only with thine eyes"? I should like to hear you sing that to me.

I dare say you will find the book of the "in-laws" interesting, but I could not give you a complete list of the nephews & nieces – and I am not quite sure whether I have told you how many of my brothers & sisters are grandfathers & grandmothers. "Rolls" is an old family name which some of us have had tacked on to us. I believe we are some connection of Lord Llangattock, whose family also have "Rolls" as their surname, but we don't know them.[12] The family split & drifted apart many, many years ago before I was thought of – so I've been told.

You dear darling frightened little mouse. So, your heart went thump when I chaffed you & wrote that I had a <u>very</u> serious question to ask you. Come into my arms and be kissed, and I promise not to frighten you anymore. Would you like that? I would just like to give you such a hug & a squeeze at this minute.

I enclose a copy of a piece of poetry I found hanging up in the Chateau I am now in. The O.B.E. (order of the British Empire) was distributed anyhow to anybody – hence these rhymes, but I dont know who the author was – I hope it won't shock you.[13]

Now I must stop & answer some of my other letters.

God bless you, dearest little sweetheart. All my love (any spare for the family)

Your devoted Reggie

<hr>

64. (31.8.18)

B.E.F.
31.8.18

Dearest Darling,

I will begin another letter to you, and leave it open till the post arrives, <u>in case</u> it should bring a letter from you. I hope you are quite, <u>quite</u> well now, cold quite gone, and no headache left. I have been so busy answering all my letters of congratulation. You never saw such a pile of letters as arrived by yesterday's post – My staff grinned at me when the post came in, so I told them they would know what to expect when <u>their</u> turn came.

I hope you won the table decorating competition. I am sure you have good taste, & the two little hearts of mauve must have looked very sweet. I always keep your <u>last</u> letter, until the next one arrives – I cannot keep them all, or I should require an extra waggon to cart them about. I hope my best beloved doesn't mind – I remember the contents pretty well, and think you are the dearest darling in the whole world to say you could not believe you could miss anyone so much as you miss your Reggie. You <u>ARE</u> a darling to care for me so much. I woke <u>up</u> early this morning and my first thoughts on waking were of you; and I just

<hr>

12 Father of Charles Rolls of Rolls Royce fame who was killed in a 1910 flying mishap. RH's paternal Grandmother was Ann Rolls (1785-1862).

13 The OBE was instituted in 1916 as an award for service to the nation. There were various versions of dismissive refrain: "Other Bloke's/Bugger's Efforts" or "Own Bloody Efforts".

<u>did</u> wish you were by my side. I long to hold my little sweetheart in my arms, and to fondle and caress her, for I love her so, and I want her so, and no one else will do – and I seem to love you more and more every day, and to want you more and more every day.

I enclose a report on a Club for Working Girls in Lambeth, founded by two of my sisters (Bee and Ivy) over 30 years ago – with the object of giving the factory girls round Lambeth somewhere to go in the evening, instead of having only the streets to walk about in.

From being quite a small affair, it has grown to be one of the most successful and best run clubs of its kind, and actually got the prize for being the best club for Working Girls in London.[14]

My sister Bee spent a large proportion of her income on it, and when she died she endowed it, so as to make sure of keeping it going. Ivy has been Her Treasurer for years & visits the club regularly.

What we want is regular <u>annual</u> subscribers, to ensure a regular <u>income</u> coming in to the club, so that it will not be dependent on chance donations, which are so variable. When you have time look through it. There's no hurry about it. If it appeals to you, perhaps you could get a few small annual subscribers to keep it along with a regular subscription, no matter how small – Every little helps – Your letter of 27th just came – But we've got orders to be moving again, so I must "get busy".

All my love to my darling little sweetheart, from her Devoted <u>Reggie</u>

65. (3.9.18)

I return the enclosed charming letter from your Aunt – and hope I shall one day meet her – She must be a <u>dear</u> like her niece Violet <u>She</u> is the dearest of all.

B.E.F.
Sept 3rd

My Darling,
I am writing this in what was a German front line trench 2 days ago, and unburied dead Bosches are lying out still unburied – Very gruesome. I received a dear letter from you yesterday, in this captured trench – Isn't our post wonderful? But I am hard put to find time to write to my Darling, & I'm sorry you have not heard from me for 3 days or more – I've not had my boots off or undressed since my last letter, but managed a shave and an apology for a wash this morning after I had been round my Battn & cheered my fellows up after a rough handling which they got from a Bosch counter attack yesterday, in which I had a good many casualties. However, the general advance made during the day was splendid, and all goes well, and the Bosch keeps returning.

I was set to do a very ambitious task yesterday, and as I expected, the Bosch counter attack was too strong for my lads, and they failed to get as far forward as they were asked to get. We found the Bosch in greater strength that was expected. We captured about 10 guns, & a lot of machine guns, we had some hard fighting.

I slept like a log last night and am very fit and well. So glad to hear your cold is so much

---

14   The club folded as a result of post-1918 women becoming emancipated.

better. Take care of yourself – sleep well & promise me not to worry if you don't hear from me – I <u>must try</u> and concentrate all my thoughts on my work, and not let my <u>great</u> love for you hinder me in it.

You have all my love my dearest darling, and I <u>yearn</u> to see you again.

Always

Your loving and devoted

Reggie.

66. (5.9. 18)

B.E.F.
5.9.18

Please send me a packet of envelopes, or you'll get no more letters from me. There's a horrid threat for you.

My dearest Darling,

Here's a few more lines for you written in the same trench not 1000 miles from Peronne, and I was pleased – Oh. So pleased – to get another letter from you. I shall never get tired of seeing my darlings' handwriting, and I think it is such nice clear writing too.

I told you we had had hard fighting, as the Bosch put up a stronger resistance than had been expected, but today things have gone smoothly and well. We all had to wear our gas masks for an hour last night just as I was turning in, as the Bosch put a lot of gas shells near us, which however did not affect us till the wind changed, which it did for about an hour. After that it changed back again, and we took off our horrid masks, & went to bed in our boots as usual.

<u>Yes</u>, I have been busy too in my spare (?) time replying to letters of congratulation and am gradually working them off. I am so glad my darling has had so many. What a popular little flower my Violet is – <u>My</u> Violet. My darling little flower. I am afraid I can give you no idea <u>at present</u> when I am likely to get leave. I can only suggest your father accepting any offer he gets for 49 Charles St, and if its let, its let, and we <u>must</u> get married from another house – or Ruckley. Perhaps my eldest brother might come to the rescue by putting you all up at his house 48 Mount St, & I could go to my sisters flat; but I am afraid it's impossible to settle anything definitely at present. You are <u>not</u> a forward girl suggesting dates – You are a darling, and I'd like to marry you tomorrow if I could and stop <u>our</u> "great big yearning". I wish I could fix a date with any certainty, but I cannot at present, as I am in the thick of the fray. We must abide in patience (<u>and</u> in love please.) and I can only repeat what I said to you <u>years</u> ago, when I took both your hands in mine at Ruckley, looked straight in to your eyes and said "D—n this war." I wish I could look straight in to your eyes at this minute – Such nice eyes my Violet has got – and see an answering gleam in them, then my arms would go round you, & I'd give my darling some very loving kisses which I feel sure she would return me. I think she has a charming sympathetic and responsive nature, and that we are perfectly "in tune", and long may we remain so, Discords must be kissed away. – when they come – But I hope the day is far far distant when there will be any dischord – (or is it discord – I am sure its chord). Now I must stop this – Its quite a long letter – written in the open air,

after a lovely day with plenty of sun – I've seen a few scared partridges flying about, but the ground is all shell holes, weeds & wire entanglements, and every village is deserted and in ruins – I have not seen a single inhabitant since we passed through Albert 3 days ago, & there were none there.

So glad the cold is so much better. You never even mentioned it – and I hope the appetite and "sleep-itite" [sic] is good too.

Take care of yourself my darling, for the sake of your devoted Reggie who loves you – Mind you let me know of any change of your address long beforehand or you'll miss my letters.

❧ ☙

67. (5.9.18)

B.E.F.

Sept 5"

Darling – My Darling,

Here's a few more lines for you to tell you that all's well – I left the German trench this morning in which I had been sleeping on the ground, and got back into reserve, which means that I am in a rabbit hutch of a place further back, and have had a bath and change, and I feel as fit as a fiddlestring.

We pushed through Moislains yesterday and are now to the East of that place. My sister Ivy tells me she has had such a nice letter from you – Thank you darling, for writing to her so nicely. No letter from you this morning, but I dare say I shall get one this afternoon as I hear there is a mail for us – only this leaves first, so I shall be unable to answer yours.

Sybil Hoare, my brother Arthurs' wife, has also written to you I hear.

It may interest you to hear that I have had your dear little "hanky" & some white heather in my pocket all through these last days, and ever since I left you – and as I have been sleeping in my clothes it has been very near me. Tonight, I hope to get into pyjamas and sleep in my camp bed. But I have slept splendidly the last few nights inspite [sic] of a lot of artillery fire quite close by.

When you have nothing else to write about, write me the history of your love for this Reggie of yours – Chap: I. How you were first attracted – Because I suppose I must have "attracted" you in some way. Chap II. How and when you first discovered that I was "rather nice" – or that you first found you liked me. Chap III. How and why that liking began to grow, & what made it grow into something stronger.

What made you keep my photo on your table? It was very dear of you to do that all the time I was away, but what made you do it? And I hear mine was the only man's photo on your table. Bless you, darling. And then my darling took to sending me socks she had knitted herself, and other nice things. Violet, you are a PEARL. Come here and be kissed. You darling, you darling, you darling. Thats what I am feeling like at this minute. Now to talk sensibly – About our wedding I can only advise you to get everything ready for it, so that when I do come home, we can be married quite soon. I shall have no trousseau – But I am writing to my tailors to have a special new jacket made for me to be married in. Possibly in another 10 days' time I may be able to tell you with more certainty when I am likely to get home, but at present I cannot do so. Times out here are much too stirring for me to be able to fix any date, but I should <u>think</u> I might get home about the middle or end of October. But you must try and not be disappointed if I cannot get home till later.

In the meantime, my PEARL must take care of herself, so that when her Reggie does get home he will find her "jumping for joy", and bursting with rude health. absolutely "pulling double".

No more now. God for ever bless and keep you.

Always your loving, and devoted Reggie

68. (7.9.18)

B.E.F.
7.9.18

My Darling,

We are still moving on chasing the retreating Bosch, & all goes well – I did not until yesterday, as I had a long & tiring day & hoped for an easy today, but we got sudden orders to push on – Now I've just got in (7.40 pm) & find your dear letter and must answer it, as I am afraid you are worrying about the house question – Of course we won't take one for the honeymoon – I've told my family we are open to offers for the loan of a house or flat in London, or a house in the country for our honeymoon – and told them not to all speak at once. No one has got any servants, so it could be a real picnic. even if we could get the loan of a house, which I think is very doubtful.

Its "up to me", I suppose, to find a home for my Darling little brown mouse, but if she says she doesn't want a home till I can get home for good – right oh. But there's no harm in keeping an eye on advertisements, in case you hear of a suitable house – and that is all I really meant when I wrote "look out for a house" – "any old place" with my Darling will suit me & Whitchurch, Salop sounds quite all right – What about Derbyshire & the Meynell country? Gradually we'll find out where there are houses, and where we will <u>not</u> go – Did my Darling think I was scolding her, or going to scold her? <u>Darling, Darling,</u> I couldn't do that. Just come here. Now do as you are told: put your arms round me, – (and there would come about a hundred and fifty of the very "bestest" nicest, "lovingest" kisses I could give you). That's the only kind of scolding I'd like to give you – Would like to be "scolded" again like that? All right. I am quite ready. I can quite see that it would be horrid to leave you alone in a house after I (perhaps) had to come back to this country again, but I hoped that what with your relations and many friends, helped by the "in-laws", you would never be alone for long, and then when I came home. again, I should find my Darling with a "nest for rest" for me to come to – a home for us both which my Darling has got ready. It's a sort of "Castle in the air" which I had built, but I quite see the difficulties, and it shall be just as you wish. We must put up with Hotels for a bit. I did not think it <u>possible</u> for us to have any <u>home</u> for our honeymoon. But the idea of a sort of hurried wedding aux all too short honeymoon, and then you go back to your family again afterwards didn't seem to me to be at all the ideal arrangement, what <u>you</u> would like, or what <u>I</u> should like. Only I didn't see what other arrangement is possible. I <u>do</u> want to make you happy <u>and comfortable,</u> and I have seen a lot of the discomfort which soldiers' wives have to put up with, and I should like to prevent my Darling having <u>any</u> discomfort to put up with, if I could manage it. It's only my concern for you, which made me write about a house.

Thank you so much for the photos of yourself. I love these photos of you, & if you've got another one of them just write "Violet" across it in your own handwriting, & <u>that's</u> the one I'll put in the dear little frame which you also sent.

No, please don't go in for <u>continuous</u> cooking or nursing – I didn't like the idea of you doing either, but we've all got to do a bit in this war, and I like to think you are doing your little bit. I would not like you to be doing nothing, so long as you are strong enough, but if you go knocking yourself up doing too much, I'll <u>forbid</u> you – yes, <u>forbid</u> you (come and be kissed.) to do any more. You have become very <u>precious</u> to me, and so I hope you'll take care of yourself & not try & do too much.

You sent me an advt. of a house near Haselmere – I enclose another – I don't fancy Haslemere, though the county round there is lovely & we took "Blackdown" near there some years ago. But Haslemere itself is rather suburban now, and much built over.

<u>After dinner</u> – at which I drank your health – so my darling thinks she's rather shy and reserved – Perhaps I think thats one of her charming attributes – But I hope she won't be shy and reserved with me – Just be your own dear self, confide in me, trust in me, and "let yourself go" with me, so that we get to know each other better and better – I'll respect your confidence, and I'll love you for your trust in me, and we shall be the best of pals, because we shall know each other thoroughly, and so <u>understand</u> each other. Show me your real feelings either in writing, if we are separated, or by your actions when we are together. I am confident that my Darling has a very strong disposition, and I wish she was here at this minute, and believe she would give me proof of it, by coming and kissing me. <u>How</u> I would return your kisses, and hold you <u>close</u> to me in a very comfy embrace – (This sort of thing is giving me an attack of the "dithers.", and I got them badly two nights ago when I lay awake thinking of you and longing for you). Yes, we both had them that evening in the drawing room, and I found it – as I told you – very intoxicating. Just write me your thoughts and feelings when you feel you have any particular thoughts or feelings you'd like to tell me about, and I shall love and respect your confidences. I think the way we write to each other is charming. How I wish I could <u>say</u> all I feel – Write to me openly and frankly, and don't be afraid of "letting yourself go" when writing, if you feel like it.

So sorry dear old Mon got a letter of "congrats" intended for you – My sympathy & love to her – She's a brick, and I hope she'll find a nice man for a husband, & be <u>supremely</u> happy, as I trust we shall be.

I'll see about a Regtl Badge brooch for you when I get home, & the plain gold ring which you want I presume is the wedding ring. What fun we shall have when are married, and how I shall chaff my little "mate". It will be a "life sentence" you know. Can you really feel that you can face that? You can? You <u>absolute perfect Darling</u>. Come and be kissed again.

Now I must go my little camp bed – It's a very small one, but how I wish I could see your dear face looking at me, and you holding out your arms to me, and hear you saying, "Come and love me Reggie Darling". I am sure this sort of a letter is bad for you – & I ought not to write like this – What do you think? But I am so <u>yearning</u> for you. Such a great big "Yearn".

The Horrid Bosches have destroyed all the pumps, and wells in the Villages, and we are experiencing great difficulty in getting a water supply as we move along.

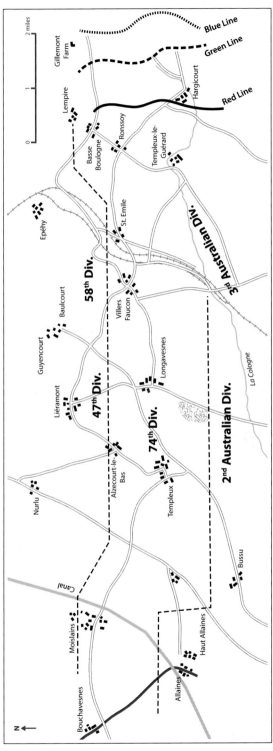

The advance from Bouchavesnes, September 1918: Brigadier-General Hoare was wounded during these operations.

I today rode out to Longuaresnes (look at a map in The Times) and from there could see Villers Fancon, Roisel & Templeux in the distance.

All my love to my Darling – (any you don't want, give to the family) – God for ever bless & keep you safe, and free from all harm – Good night.

Beloved.

Your devoted Reggie.

～⊘～

69. (9.9.18)

B.E.F.

9.9.18

In a Red X Hospital train

Darling,

I'm all right. It was silly of me to get in the way of a Bosch shell. And it was <u>very</u> careless of the Bosch to have selected your Reggie.

This is how it happened. I was riding out at 7.30am this morning to go round my line, as my little lot are in the front line again. I had got a mile on my way, when a shell arrived and pitched halfway between my orderly and myself – He was riding about 10 or 15 yards behind me. Crash. and I felt my horse stagger, & I felt as if someone had hit me with half a brick in the small of the back.

My orderly shouted out his horse was hit – so was mine, but I made the orderly ride him on with me to one side, out of the line the shell came from, & then we both dismounted and led our horses back. My horse was hit by fragments in 3 or 4 places, and I have been hit by fragments in 2 or 3 places. Back of right shoulder blade, & small of the back, left side, I felt none the worse, and wanted to get another horse & go out again, after I had had the places attended to, but the Drs insisted on my becoming a casualty as there are pieces still in me they think, so here I am, en route to Rouen in a hospital train. <u>Very</u> stiff and sore now. I refused to be a lying down case and crept along like a <u>Very</u> old man to the train, but I think I shall be lying down when I get to my Base Hospital at Rouen.

What will happen there I don't know; they may decide that its not serious enough to send me home. On the other hand, if it's going to be a month or 6 weeks job, they probably <u>will</u> send me home – I am <u>so</u> sorry Darling for giving you such a fright. But you nearly lost your Reggie, and he is very lucky to get off so cheaply. "Don't worry any" – Don't write or wire, or do anything till you hear from me again, and I know what they are going to do with me – All is well – I quite <u>expect</u> to be sent home, and if so, I shall say "Thank you Mr Bosche for so kindly arranging for me to see my Darling again so soon".

Here you see one of the troubles which a soldiers' wife will have to face. I trust my darling is facing it bravely, but there is nothing to worry about. I shall soon be up and about again when the stiffness & soreness goes off.

All my love

Your Reggie.

～⊘～

Hospital and Blighty

70. (10.9.18)

Rouen,
10.9.18

It's all right Darling; they are sending me home tonight via Havre & Southampton, & I shall be quite comf. in a hospital in London by the time this reaches you.

They have X-rayed me & I've got 3 small bits of shell in the small of my back, & which the surgeon here says might just as well stay where they are unless they give trouble, then they will have to be taken out. The Gash over my right shoulder blade is ugly to look at and will take time to heel. It will be altogether a month or 6 weeks job. I shall try & get to 17 Park Lane Hospital – or a hospital in Grosvenor Place where I can get a room to myself.

I feel very stiff & sore (as if I'd had a bad toss out hunting & my horse had rolled over me 2 or 3 times). But I shall soon be up and about again – and I hope if you come south we shall have some long talks together.

I shall leave word at the Naval & Military Club, 94 Piccadilly, what hospital I am in.

I am so sorry if I have frightened my Darling – Its was very careless of the Bosch gunner to have picked me out, but my beauty (!) is unimpaired, and it might have been much worse.

All my love to my Darling and I hope she is not worrying – so looking forward to seeing you again, but you are not to come rushing down on purpose to see Your devoted

Reggie

⁘

71.(12.9.18)

17, Park Lane, W.1.
12"

My Darling,

Here I am, comfortably settled in a room to myself, and I feel tons better already – I quite expect to mend up again quite quickly and be running and jumping about like a 2-year-old before the month is out. I had to stop in the middle of this as Lady Somerleyton, who is nursing here, came in to see me – I have known her for many years, but did not know she was here – I was told Lady (Merrick) Banerly was nursing here, but she is not.

Well, I had a good crossing on a very fine Hospital Ship, the _____ (Hush).

Castle, and there were 600 wounded on board, and a few Bosch wounded too, and I got here at about 3 pm – Not bad going – Hit at 7.30 AM on 9th, and in bed in a London Hospital by 3pm 12th. Of course, I've missed lots of your dear letters. I wonder where you are & what you are doing – I hope you won't think it necessary to come down here all in a hurry just because your Reggie has got a few scratches. But you may send him some grouse with your love, as often as you like.

I am oh! so fit and well already, but I shall not know whether they intend to operate on me or not till tomorrow. I don't think they will do so. Anyhow digging out a few bits of metal won't be much of an operation.

I feel I am going to see you soon – I do so wonder how soon. And I am so looking forward to seeing my Darling – I am almost inclined to say "Bless the Bosch for giving me such a nice comfortable wound, so that I can come home & see my Darling again.

My brother from Mount St has just come in to see me, so I must stop.

All my love to my Darling

Your devoted

Reggie

Will it give you a shock to see me in bed? But perhaps I shall be up and about.

72. (13.9.18)[15]

> Sweetheart I love you so
> At Sea
> 5pm

Dearest Darling, you'll be getting quite tired of the sight of my "pothooks" and handwriting, but there will be a gap in my letters after this, as I shall not have so much time for letter writing. I do so wonder how you are feeling, and whether you are missing your Reggie <u>very</u> much. I think you had got to like him just a little bit. You darling girl – Hadn't you?

I am "O.C. Ship" and am sitting in a very special cabin reserved for me, with my lifebelt on, and everyone else has got one on too. How I wish you were here with me. It has been a perfect day, (only as regards the weather – absolutely <u>rotten</u> in other respects), glorious sunshine – a very smooth sea. Its rotten to think that if I could only have found out the time the boat went, I could have stayed another day at Cabrach. But it's no good worrying about that now. "Pack up your troubles in your old Kitbag and <u>smile, smile, smile</u>." That's the song I want you to get, & to learn, please will you? I just <u>love</u> your smile – <u>are you smiling?</u> Let me know if you like the Lily of the Valley scent which I sent better than what you use – I like yours <u>awfully</u>, because <u>it's yours</u>, & it reminds me of you & nobody else – Don't change unless <u>you prefer</u> what I sent.

Well, the weeks will soon fly by, and I hope soon to see you again, so keep "merry and bright", and take care of yourself for the sake of your Reggie who loves you <u>very</u>, <u>very</u> devotedly.

I hope you will be able to write me nice cheerful letters, such as a soldiers wife, (which please God you are soon to be), should write her husband, and please answer anything in the form of a question which I may have asked you in my letters, so that we can keep a conversation going so to speak. I wonder if you will "spot" anything in this letter. Read the first page <u>very</u> carefully and tell me what you find there.

You will know this is posted in France because there will be no stamp on it.

You must have had enough of my drivelling letters by now, but I could go on writing like this for hours to you, because you are <u>my</u> darling, and I think you are beginning to realise now <u>how</u> much I care for you – I am only just finding it for myself how awfully in love I am with you. I just love you, <u>love you love you</u>, & I pray God to bless you & keep you safe till I return.

---

15   This letter may have followed the one dated 23 August 1918, as it was obviously written on the return boat back to France following RH's leave. Posted immediately on arrival, it must have gone astray!

<u>Always</u> your devoted & loving
Reggie

⚘

73. (13.9.18)

17 Park Lane
14.1.
13.9.18

My Darling,

All goes well – I've had my scratches dressed. The chief surgeon here has examined them and decided to leave them for a few days and see how they go on. If they heal up all right, and I do not mind carrying about a little extra weight in the shape of a few fragments of shell which have lodged in my back, he will not operate at all, but "let sleeping dogs lie". So that's how the matter stands at present.

I have been out of bed and sitting up all the morning, so you can now realise what a fraud I am to be in England at all – "Rotten Cotten Reggie". My sister Ivy has been to see me this morning and is coming again this afternoon. She tells me she has heard from you, and I think I have written to you every day since I was hit. I hope you have had the letters. It seems <u>ages</u> since I last heard from you, but of course it cannot be helped as I've been travelling so fast – but I've been <u>hungry</u> – oh so <u>hungry</u> – for a letter from my Darling for the last 5 days – I was hit on the morning of 9th and hacked off at once.

And how is my Darling? Has she been worrying much about her Reggie? I hope my wire & letters have been sufficiently reassuring to prevent you thinking my scratches were in any way serious, but I was so afraid lest you should receive a horrid shock by seeing a horrid bald statement in the papers before hearing from me all about it. It has not appeared in print yet. It's worth getting wounded if I'm going to *see* you again soon – You can come here any day, and every day, and twice a day, & we'll have some nice talks together. If the wounds go on all right I shall be allowed out of doors in a couple of days' time & then we can sit in the Park, or I'll motor you to Hurlingham or Ranelagh or anywhere you like – Only I cannot do much walking just yet.

So glad to see Invincible has won a race, and I hope your father put something on for me. I told him that my winning would be expended in a present for you.

By the bye, I meant to have brought you something else when I was last in London. Can you guess what? It was some nice hatpins, to make up for the poor hatpin who lost his head, when we both lost our heads (and hearts) to each other on a certain Sunday afternoon – Happy day.

Now I must stop this to catch the post. All my love to my best beloved, from your devoted Reggie

⚘

74. (14.9.18)

17 Park Lane
14"

No, dearest Darling, you are <u>not</u> to come round and see me tonight, You would not be allowed in, so it's no good your trying – And even if it were not long "after hours", I should still say "No" much as I long to see your dear face again – But you have had a long & tiring journey, & are to go to bed, and sleep & rest, & come round & see me in the morning – Ivy will call for you, but you must not get here before 11.30 A.M. & that's really too early – I am writing this at 11.AM, & have not been dressed – my scratches I mean – yet, but I've had my bath & "brek", and am sitting up in a chair.

It's quite likely your train will be an hour late or more – And as far as I can make out you are travelling alone – <u>How</u> I wish I was with you – My darling will arrive very tired and worried, and I dont know what she has done for dinner, but I have ordered them to have <u>something</u> ready for you so that you won't quite starve. And I hope you will like the flowers which I send with my very best love. Now go to bed like a good girl, and <u>sleep</u>. I'd like to kiss you to <u>sleep</u>. You must take the will for the deed and <u>sleep</u> and come round in the morning after a good night's rest & you'll find your Reggie oh <u>so</u> well, & <u>so</u> pleased to see you.

If your train had got in at 4pm, 5pm, or 6pm – I should have come & met you myself. That will show you how well I am – All my love to my Darling –Your devoted Reggie

You'll see him in the morning.

75. (21.9.18)

"Bensons"
25, Old Bond Street,
London.W.1.
21st

I hope you will like this – if not, don't hesitate to say so, & I'll get it changed. Its not <u>half</u> good enough for you, but it's an <u>uncut</u> emerald, and for some reason that made me prefer it to a cut stone. You asked me for an emerald. I felt like buying you the whole shop.

With <u>all</u> my love to my darling from Reggie

I leave London 8.AM. tomorrow for Dover.

[On separate card]
I remember your saying you liked Green Jade. Here's a bit with my best love for my best beloved.

I am also sending you some Lavender Soap to try. Please try the biggest pieces first – I think they are the best.

<u>Your Reggie</u>

76. (23.9.18)
Telegrams, Whitegate.
Stations, Whitegate.

Cheshire Lines,
Midland Railway &
Hartford, L & N W Railway
Telephone 16 Sandiway
Cassia,
Winsford,
Cheshire
Friday

Dearest one,

<u>So</u> glad to hear from you this morning, and to learn that all goes well – You will be glad to be up in a chair on Sunday, but I hope you won't be very disappointed with yourself and feel very tired afterwards.

I wonder whether Rea is right in saying the daughter will not be operated on for <u>6 weeks</u>. I understood Legge to say in a few <u>days</u>. I should ask Dr Legge about it.

Very windy all yesterday, and again a moderate days racing, but I did not find winners so lost my money.

I will find out about Zanoni – thanks for sending on the tip. I enclose P & Jones receipted bill which has reached me here. I have also had a bill from the National Fish Co:. Grimsby for <u>4/3 May 31st.</u> I will send them a P.O.

Is Miss Rea to stay with her parents or going back to her place? There is a Beckbury carrier who goes in to Shipnal regularly I believe – Rea should make use of that or buy a motor for himself.

Take care of yourself my Darling – All my love
Your devoted husband,[16]
Reggie

77. (10.10.18)

Gorse Cottage
Crawley Down
10th

My dearest Darling,

I did not feel so far away from you this morning when I heard your dear voice on the phone – But oh, how I hated going away from you yesterday. However family ties, & engagements must not be ignored, and once made, I stick to them, unless the family tell me not to come – I should have loved the partridge shoot at Newmarket, but I would not disappoint my sisters – and they won't see much of me after the 24th, will they? so I had made up my mind to "shed the light of my countenance" on them this week, and then they cannot say "we never see anything of Reggie when he is at home". And we are really a very united family for

16   This letter appears out of sequence and following their marriage, R.H. signed himself "Your devoted husband". I suspect Violet was poorly at Ruckley and the bill from National Fish Co., Grimsby, 31 May suggests a fishing trip to Scotland with the consequent catch sent off for smoking.

such a large one, & very fond of each other.

And now what shall I write about. I can only think of telling you again of my <u>great</u> love for you, which seems to grow greater every day. I found out how much I cared (and perhaps you realised it a bit too) when I saw you rather tired & overdone the other evening, because I had not been with you to take care of you, & <u>cherish</u> you, and to see that my Darling did not attempt too much, and did her shopping more comfortably. It was a very long day for you, and my concern for you was very great that evening. I longed to be <u>alone with you</u>, and I really enjoyed driving about in the coupe with you on my knee more than the evening before – We seemed such good pals, & I loved your coming & taking an interest in my suits & trying on. You are the dearest Darling in the whole world – There – thats how I feel about you. Do you like that?

This is a dear little cottage, and I wish you were here with me – only 14 more days and then.

I have given the Rev: the Honble. Campbell Douglas your London address, so don't be surprised if he calls on you. I told him you might like to meet him before the ceremony, then you would not feel quite so much as if you were being married by a stranger.

I hope to meet him at Aldershot on Sunday too. Would you like the "address" at the end of the marriage service cut out altogether, if so I think it can be done – It's a long-winded affair – read it through and tell me. In its place a <u>few</u> words can be said by one of the clergymen, or that part can be dispensed with altogether I believe – Let me know what you'd like and tell me when next we meet.

Next item please. Your bridal bouquet. White flowers of course – Any particular likes or dislikes? All white carnations – or carnations, white roses & orange blossom if the latter can be got – and the shape? round – or sheaf like? and is there any particular florist you'd like it from?

Has your mother <u>definitely</u> decided to be responsible for the bridesmaids' bouquets? If not, you must come write me and order them, to go with their dresses. They are usually the gifts of the Bridegroom, & I don't want to shirk any of my responsibilities.

Very warm and summer-like here this morning, after a good deal of rain in the night, but it has clouded over now, & looks like being wet again.

I wonder if you will go to Tong church on Sunday & hear the banns read there. It would do you no harm to have a really quiet and lazy day, and a good rest after all the racketing about you've had in London.

I hope the old Rector has made good improvement, and looks like getting over his stroke – All my love to my Darling from her devoted Reggie

※ ②〆

78. (11.10.18)
Station, Witley.

Matteryes,
Hambledon,
Surrey. Oct: 11"

Dearest One,
Many thanks for your letter which arrived here half an hour after I did.

Bless you for saying you missed me so. Well, it won't be very long now before we shall be together for a very long time, and if I "starve" you then, you must let me know. But I don't think that's likely to happen. I trust my Darling will be very, very happy for <u>years, and years, and years.</u>

I hope you will have a good rest while at home.

I shall so look forward to seeing you again.

All my love

Your devoted

Reggie.

79. (12.10.18) Two short notes:

Station, Witley.

Muriel is sending me a silver salver, so bear that in mind, tho we want more than one.

Matteryes,

Hambledon,

Surrey.

<u>12"</u>

My Darling,

Such a lovely morning here; glorious view from this house over beautiful scenery, & I wish you were here to go out for a ramble with me. I hope you had a comfy journey home, and have slept well, and are enjoying a good rest.

Will you lunch at 48 Mount St on Wednesday next at 1.30, and meet my niece Mrs Loder. I shall be there. Muriel Loder is a widow whose husband was killed in Palestine.

Will you send a reply direct to Mrs Rolls Hoare at 48 Mount St. as she will like to know beforehand, & I may not arrive up till Wednesday morning.

I go to Aldershot this afternoon, & to Beenham on Monday, returning to London Wednesday morning – Post just going – All my love to my dearest darling – Your devoted Reggie

80. (autumn 1918, month undetermined)

17 Park Lane, W.1.

21st[17]

My Darling,

The enclosed explains itself, though nothing is said about horses to ride, which was a question I had asked – However, I'm pretty certain theres nothing there beyond a couple of ponies which go in the governess cart, so don't bother to bring your habit. We'll take a little gentle walking exercise or motoring instead.

I am just back from a very cheery lunch at the Savoy with Col. & Mrs Winch (Scots

---

17   This would seem to precede letter 74 from hospital, i.e., prior to RH's voyage to Dover.

Greys), and Cap & Mrs Bampfylde. Col. Winch was my Bde Major for a time in Egypt, & George Bampfylde was my A.D.C. at the beginning of the war, and afterwards became my Staff Captain, but could not stand the Climate of Palestine & had to go home sick – Both are now doing staff work with the Air Force in London – Mrs Bampfylde has asked me to bring you to dine with them when we are next in London together.

I do so hope you are having a comfy journey and don't find yourself very tired after all the dissipation we have had together in town. I have just loved every minute of it, and London does seem <u>so</u> empty now without my Darling.

I've just had a talk to the Matron, and I have to go before a board again on Monday. I think the Board only mean to give me the extra week sick leave which they did me out of by making me attend the last Board while I was still in Hospital. Anyhow I will wire you the result of the Board on Monday.

Sister said my shoulder looked <u>much</u> cleaner & better this morning, though she added she thought it would want proper dressing after Tuesday – We shall see – No dressing on my back today.

I enclose some more advts of house. You will see one is in Shropshire, though I don't know where Church Stretton is, & the Rector does not say how many rooms his Rectory has – though its "small".

I love my locket & have got it on now strung on by a bit of black string like an eye glass string.

Aldermaston is your station for Tuesday; Look out for my "Brass hat" at Reading as I shall be travelling in uniform, as it's cheaper.

Mrs Bampfylde who knows Devonshire well says hunting <u>will</u> be 'going on, but it may be ----------- hunting. She advises us to get married <u>in the morning</u> & leave by the 1.pm train, arriving about 6.pm.

All my love to my Darling & I hope you'll sleep well, and rest all you can. <u>Bless you.</u> <u>Bless you. Bless you</u>

Your Reggie

P.S.

The enclosed has come since my other letter was written. Please yourself about the habit. It's only a small pony for you, and Jenny is an old Boer pony, over 20 years old, incapable of any fast pace, but I expect my back would not stand a fast gallop – "Bingham" is the groom.

I don't know Bucklebury Common, but it sounds inviting, & I'd love to ride with you, and I think perhaps my Violet would rather like a ride with her devoted & loving <u>Reggie</u>

You were just rec'd. Many thanks, so glad you've had a comfy journey.

81. (13.10.18)

I hope you have had a good rest while away, & a comfy journey <u>back.</u>

Aldershot
Sunday evening.

Dearest one,

Thank you ever so much for your letter written in the train – It was dear of you to have written in the train, because I feel sure it was not easy, or comfortable – But it's a sweet letter, & I love it, <u>and</u> the writer.

I shall address this to 49, in case it's not catching you at Ruckley if you leave by the early train.

Now to clear up a little business:

1. I hope to meet you at lunch at 48 Mount St, at 1.30. I shall get there a little before that hour if I can, so as to get a few minutes alone with my darling if possible, supposing I don't see her before. I shall arrive Paddington at 10.45 on Wednesday morning, and shall ask my brother to send his car to meet me – Don't know whether he will – But I expect so. I shall drop my luggage at Mount St., & then go on shopping in the Car, & will call for you at 49 at any hour you like – after 11.15, & we can go shopping or trying on together if you like.

2. But I expect you've got a lot of appointments to keep & will do it better & quicker without me. But I'll call for you at 49 at 1.P.M. anyhow, & bring you to lunch, (unless you are already engaged for lunch), & we might go out together afterwards in brother's car.

3. Bertie & Mrs Bertie want to give us a china (sort of "Spood") breakfast service. Have you already had one promised? if not, I shall say yes, & will show you the pattern at Goodes (S. Audley St.).

4. Both my Chaplains are coming up to assist in the wedding service. So, there will be no lack of parsons.[18]

5. I am in favour of dining with Lady Clarke on Wednesday night, & will call for you, & bring you home again.[19]

6. I am getting a copy of our old Regimental march, so we need not listen to the dreadfully hackneyed "Wedding March".

There that ends all the "business". I <u>loved</u> the way you ended up your letter. Do you know, darling, I had <u>such</u> a long talk to you this morning in bed, when I woke up. You seemed to be near me, & I seemed to be talking to you. It was rather an affectionate sort of conversation, & you seemed to be in a responsive mood, and I felt quite "dithery" at last. <u>How</u> I wish you had been there. I wonder if you ever have those sort of conversations (in imagination) to me – Perhaps you do, & that <u>that's</u> what keeps you awake sometimes.

I go to Beenham tomorrow for Monday night – shoot about 10 pheasants, & I leave (perhaps) on Tuesday, & leave there by a 9.30 AM train on Wednesday morning arriving Padd: 10.45.

---

18   The chaplains were Revd. W.G. Pennyman and Revd. the Hon. L.C.H Campbell-Douglas, CF.

19   Lady Clarke (d. 1922) was the wife of Gen. Sir Charles Mansfield Clarke (1839-1932), an old friend from India. He was C-in-C Madras Army 1893, GOC II Corps South Africa,1899, QMG 1899-1903, Governor of Malta 1903-07.

I expect you will be out, busy shopping, so shan't expect to see you till 1. o'clock, but send a line to me at 48 Mount St., telling me what you will be doing. It seems ages & ages since I last saw you, and the feeling I have is that I simply must see my Darling, the Very minute I arrive in London; but that feeling is only natural, because I love you and it won't hurt to wait till 1.pm before seeing you, as I'm sure you've got lots to do.

I had a jolly ride with my brother over to the Long Valley & racecourse this afternoon – I wished you had been with me instead, because you are the dearest little darling in the whole world to me, and I am Your most loving & devoted Reggie

～◎ ◎～

82. (15.10.18)
Telegrams, Beenham.   Beenham Grange,
Station, Aldermaston, C.W.R.   Berkshire.
                                                                Tuesday

Dearest one,
Thank you ever so much for your letters of 12" & 13" received at Aldershot & here this morning.

My brother is better – Was downstairs yesterday and stayed up to Dinner; when we all drank your health.

I have heard of a very good hunter, which must soon be sold – the owner, "Jos" Hanbury having just died – He was late Master of the Cottesmore Hounds & always rode good horses. He was staying here with Arthur & told him this was the best hunter he ever had. Do you think your father could take it in, if I bought it? He'd have to find another man then. 8 horses would be too much for 2 men.

I have heard of 3 more presents for me. So glad you are getting such a lot, & such nice ones – You deserve them all, because you are such a darling.

The shoulder is splendid, & quite healed – only the scar left, but I am keeping on the pad & bandages until tomorrow.

I thought your mother intended to put in the paper "There will "be no reception, but all friends "will be welcome at the Church". I have heard from her that she intends to put it in next time. The same announcement was in yesterdays "Times", but D.S.O. had been omitted after my name, but that does not worry me – I have not seen any announcement that "Mr & Mrs Reid Walker have arrived at 49 Charles St, Berkeley Square", which your mother talked of putting in the papers, so as to give an address for presents – So sorry to hear you have not been sleeping so well at Ruckly – I dare say you were a bit overtired. I did not sleep well last night either – I am in your room, and rather loving thoughts of you kept me awake for some time.

So glad you can come to lunch tomorrow. My heart is singing with joy at the thought that I shall see my darling tomorrow.

Bless you for saying you have missed me. I am so looking forward to seeing you tomorrow. Tons of love from Your devoted Reggie.

～◎ ◎～

83. (17.10.18)
I will come round about 12.30.

Telegraphic Address:
Mameluke, May, London.
Telephone 6433 Mayfair (3 Lines.)

Cavalry Club
127, Piccadilly.W.1

<u>Tuesday night</u>

<u>My Dearest Darling,</u>
I have just dropped in here on my way home to write you a line, & to say how much I missed you tonight – I hope you will not have a bad time, and will take it quite, quite easy for the next few days. If there is anything I can do for you, get Mon to phone to me in the morning.

The old Lady desired me to say that she was "desolée" at your absence, and my old chief, "Sir Charles", has quite lost his heart to you, like someone else you know – I arrived v. late for dinner as I failed to get either a taxi, or the right bus, and finally commanded an electric brougham, which was going along slowly, empty.

There was no one there beside Sir Charles & Lady C., so we yarned away about old times and she dismissed me with a most touching "God bless you & I hope you & Violet will be very happy".

Good night, my dearest and best beloved, and let me know when I may see you again.
Your loving & devoted
Reggie.

Reginald and Violet on their wedding day, October 1918.

Appendix I

Hoare Family[1]

Tree: 13 of 14 children (RH 1865-1947) to Thomas Rolls Hoare 28/1/1816 – 15/1/1892. m. Emma Elizabeth Bird 6/6/1825-10/3/1909 at British Embassy, Paris 13/3/1845 with, being a minor, parental consent.

Emma 30/12/1846-22/3/1900; m. Ralph Koe (seven children.).

James Rolls 15/8/1847-10/5/1922; m Gertrude Eddison, 4 children. Nobles & Hoare partner.[2]

Alice 24/3/1849 – 27/12/1910; m. Phillip Leman.

Tom 14/3/1851-3/5/1906 u/m.

Arthur 30/11/1852-29/1/1919 m. Sybil.

Wilson 2/8/1854 – 19/1/1911 (Lt RN, OC Lt. Col. RND Yeo. 1907-1911) m. Mary Louisa Koe. (*The Times* obit. 21/1/1911.); South Africa 1899-1902, major Imperial Yeomanry; resided Warkleigh, Devon.

Grace (twin) 27/1/1856; painted by Millais as twins 1876-77; m. Rear-Admiral Sir Sidney Marow Eardley-Wilmot Kt, 1847-1929 (Superintendent Naval Ordnance Stores 1902-09. Wrote several naval articles and *An Admiral's Memories 1860-1915* (1927). Recommended an anti-torpedo bulge on Dreadnought warship hulls); 4 children.

Katie (twin) 27/1/1856 – 10/11/1948; married Admiral F.W. Gough CB (*The Times* obit. 21/1/08; Died 19/1/08.) who captained Royal Yacht *Victoria & Albert*; twins painted by

---

1   The Hoare family descended from a Richard Hoare (Hoore) who had roots in Buckinghamshire from 1430 and farmed at Great Missenden from about that time. Richard Hoare, who founded the bank that continues to this day, was born in 1648, opened his books as a goldsmith in 1673 and was Lord Mayor of London in 1713. He was 6th generation, whose junior branch farmed at Little Missenden. This cadet branch also farmed around the Wendover area of Bucks and, assuming direct lineage from Edmund, great, great grandson of Richard (1430-87) who had seven children of which Henry was the fourth son (b. circa 1571). they farmed in the vicinity of Great Missenden and Great Hamden.

2   Nobles & Hoare (est. 1787) 1-3 Cornwall Road, Stamford St., London, SE1. Charles Henry Crompton-Roberts, (1832-91), whose mother was Marianne Noble and sole heir, was supposedly the only proprietor. He was MP for Sandwich (1880-81) when the seat was annulled as voters were always bribed by both sides. High Sheriff of Monmouth, he restored and lived at Drybridge House. This suggests the Hoare family were only major shareholders. Forty employees attended his funeral. Between the wars the company lost a major Royal Navy battleship grey paint contract. Bought out by ICI, the company was renamed Dulux Paints. William Sharpington who taught me lettering at City & Guilds of London Art School 1969-72 was still employing Nobles & Hoare paint and varnish for his commissioned work.

Millais 1876.[3]

Sidney 23/7/1857-25/2/1931 m. Miss Todds-Thornton; 3 children.[4]

Ethel 7/2/1859-1/1936; m. Edward Clowes d. 1901, connected to publishing world; five children.

Mary (Bee) 7/8/1860-26/6/1916; founded and managed Club for young girls in Lambeth with Ivy until 1918; u/m.

Herbert 30/7/1863-30/1/1936. Major 5th RIDG. Wounded at Ladysmith; m. Harriet Brown; sons Neville and Archie.

Reginald 18/9/1865-/10/1947; m. Violet Eliza Reid Walker,14/5/1887-1/10/1966; children: Arthur, John (MC following D-Day, killed Malaya 1949, The Black Watch), Robin, Rosemary.

Ivy 15/9/1867- 12/5/1950. u/m.

- His niece, Gertrude Rolls (1885-1973), daughter of James Rolls Hoare; m. C.A. Baron. Their grandson Maj. Gen. Richard Baron commanded QRIH (amalgamation of 4 QORH & 8 KRIH in 1958) and Granddaughter Catherine married a QRIH officer Richard Hoare (no close relation).
- Her elder sister Muriel married Capt. Robert Loder; died of wounds First Battle of Gaza 1917, see letter 38. Their son Giles (b. 10/11/1914) succeeded Baronetcy in 1920 from grandfather who bought Leonardslee, famous for its rhododendrons, in 1887. Giles married Marie Symons-Jeune and both held RHS's Victoria Medal of Honour. They had two sons: Edmund (b. 1941) Racehorse trainer and Robin whose twins sold Leonardslee after his retirement (See letter 79, 12/10/18). She was always "Aunt Muriel" to RARH who spent much time there at post-Eton crammers for Faraday House to study electrical engineering. Also, RARH confirmed at Horsham by B.P. Bell.

Violet Eliza Reid Walker, 14/5/1887-1/10/1966: Elder daughter and eldest child of John Reid Walker (1855-1934) 2nd son of Sir Andrew Barclay Walker;[5] knighted 1887

---

3   Katie Reid Walker ran a VAD recuperation hospital at Hildern, near Shifnal, where they resided. There are some interesting entries in a book of thanks that were written by discharged patients.

4   Brothers Sidney and Herbert (see below) were often short of funds and were inclined to beg RH for a loan; no doubt he had enough funds to be a cavalry officer and play polo. Herbert had to evade the bailiffs after a mess investment scam and transferred to India.

5   Andrew Barclay Walker, 1st Baronet 1886, married firstly Eliza Reid, 16/6/1853-82, daughter of a Scottish Merchant Navy Captain John Reid, hence VH's 2nd and 3rd names; second, he married Maude Okeover, 11/10/1887 – 1943, who inherited the ancient family estate Okeover near his own at Osmarston in Derbyshire, so the senior Walker branch became Walker-Okeover, and had eight children. His eldest son Peter Carlaw Walker, 2nd Baronet, 7/5/1854-18/10/1915, married Maude's younger sister Ethel, 30/5/1899-17/3/1935. Their son Ian, 3rd Baronet, 30/11/1902-1982, commanded the Derbyshire Yeomanry in WWII winning 2 DSOs and was HML of Derbyshire after the war until 1977. In turn his

following gift of Walker Art Gallery to Liverpool; grandson of Peter Walker who founded the Walker Brewery in Warrington in 1824 and introduced a system still used today by Marstons) and Katie Howard Cartland d. 21/5/1945, youngest daughter of John Cartland, brass founder in Birmingham, whose son was the father of Barbara Cartland. John Reid Walker worked for the brewery which was the first to employ railways for deliveries beyond the range of drays and to have tied houses as a result. It was floated on the Stock Exchange, eventually bought out by Tetleys who re-instated Walker Beers in the 1980s when it also brewed the rival beer of Greenalls before closure. The landmark chimney disappeared from the scene about a decade later. He was a successful racehorse owner and breeder, besides having a polo pony stud farm. More renowned was his next younger brother Willie, created Lord Wavertree for his loan of six fillies including Minoru which won the Derby in 1907 to King Edward VII, who had the stud at Tully Co. Kildare which became successively The National Stud, until it moved to Gillingham and then Newmarket, and then The Irish National Stud. WHW also fathered a son by Violet, the illegitimate granddaughter of Edward VII and Mrs George Rayner (previously Mrs M. Gifford). This same Violet was married off to his racing manager Jack Fergusson who brought up Gordon (b 1925) as his own son with word that Willie was his Godfather from whom he inherited the estate at Sandy Brow, Cheshire. In fact, he had fathered a surrogate daughter Rosemary whom he adopted as his wife Sophie Sheridan could not have children, which no doubt made her dalliance with Edward VII in Baden-Baden easier.

John and Katie had three other children: Monica 19/2/1889-7/1/1971. Married Dennis Boles from a Somerset family 1921 (d. 1958) 17/21st Lancers but commanded the Blues Household Cavalry.; MP.

John Vincent, 1893-1974. Sectioned when 21 and remained in a home.[6]

Codrington Gwyn, 1895-1963, married 3/11/1921 his first cousin Phyllis Munro Walker, d. 1974.

---

younger daughter Jane was Lady-in-Waiting to Queen Elizabeth the Queen Mother.

6   There is a mystery here worthy of any novel, over the reason for his removal. He was born nine months after his parents were reconciled after brief estrangement when both might have had affairs, so he was not recognised as his own son by JRW who goaded him until one day the boy threatened him with a gun in the gun room. Two other possibilities are that he was either homosexual or epileptic which was a stigma to any Victorian family with social ambitions. Or he may have been bipolar which can affect people badly. His sister-in-law/first cousin told me that the person she visited in a home at Virginia Water after Gwyn died who inherited responsibility for him after their mother died was not Vincent and that she had met on a train in the war his younger double (a son?) who was in the Canadian RAF. My Mother who spent a lot of time with Katie RW, Father's Grandmother, in the early years of the war after their marriage, always said that she, Vincent's mother, had spirited him away to a new life (Canada?) and gave him an allowance because she always seemed short of money herself despite the wealth of the family, and that payments to the home were kept up as a show of his being there, especially while J.R.W. was alive.

Appendix II

Brigadier-General Reginald Hoare, CMG DSO, Military Career 1886-1918

Commissioned 4th Queen's Own Hussars, January 1886.

1893: Promoted captain and adjutant.

South Africa 1899-1902: Major ADC to Gen. Elliott. Bullet through tunic coat; promoted Lt-Col .1901-02, last six months commanded column; Capt. 4th QOH polo team that won 1899 South India Cup

1905-10: CO 4th QOH, S. Africa, Ireland, polo. *Mente et Manu* ("Mind & Hand") motto added to regimental badge by Royal Warrant 1906; RH goes on half-pay as full colonel.

12/5/1910: Completed regimental duties.

Promoted Substantive Col. TF (1912); promoted full Col (1912); TF Brigade Commander SW Mounted Brigade. Somerset Yeomanry and Devonshire Yeomanry. RH's brother, Wilson, late RN, CO RNDY 1907, dies in harness 1911.

Brig- Gen.; Brigade training, Winchester and defence of East Coast.

Camp life to Sept. 1914.

1915: 2nd Mounted Division: Training in Great Britain; bicycles; Japanese rifles utilised until issue of Lee-Enfield pattern weapons prior to embarkation for Mediterranean.

Suvla Bay 8/10/15: Too rough to disembark after transfer from SS *Olympic* to Khedive steamer *Osmanieh*; base parties at Mudros; trenches flooded 26-27 Nov. followed by snow and frost; 1st Devon Yeo. reduced to 205 effectives from 370 in one week by 29/11/15. Letter from GOC, Sir Charles Monro, Yeo of Devon. Bgd. evacuated after 11 weeks 25/12/15 without opposition from Turks.

1916: Fife & Forfar, Lanarkshire, Devon and Somerset Yeomanries operate as protective screen against Senussi Bedouins, a numerous puritanical sect of Mahommedans; Kharga to Dakhla Oasis (south of Siwa); 80-mile advance but Senussi threat had evaporated); guard training at Gara, Egypt.

31/3/16 RH home leave to Great Britain.

9/1916: Awarded Order of St Stanislaus (2nd Class with Sword), an Imperial Russian decoration in recognition of distinguished service during campaign, presumably post-Gallipoli.

1917: Creation of 74th (Yeomanry) Div. 14/1/17 (GOC Maj. Gen. E.S. Girdwood); 229th Infantry Brigade (former 2nd Dismounted Brigade): 16th Devon. Rgt., 12th Som. L.I., 12th RSF, 14th Black Watch, 4th MG Co; 74th Div. assigned to XX Corps (GOC Lt-Gen. Sir Philip Chetwode).

26/4/17: Trench digging prior to First Battle of Gaza.
Nov. 17: One of R. Hoare's chargers killed prior to Battle of Sheria.

1/7/17: Husband of RH's favourite niece Murial KIA near Gaza.

5/11/17: Attack near Beersheba at 9 a.m. and 4 p.m.; objectives achieved.

3/12/17: Battle of Foka.

8/12/17: Fierce Turkish resistance halts advance near Beit Iksa and Shafat.

9/12/17: Surrender of Jerusalem.

11/12/17: Gen Allenby dismounted entry into Jerusalem.

25/12/17: Attack on Zeitun Ridge.

28/12/17: Action near Ramallah.

Eastertide 1918: Received DSO from HRH The Duke of Connaught.

74th Division to France 7/5/18.

11/5/18: Disembarked Abbeville; marched to Rue the next day.

20/5/18: Rail journey to Roellecourt and (25 May) Le Cauroy in the Doullens area.

12th Ayr. & Lanark Battalion RSF leave 229th Bgd. to form 94th Bgd., 31st Division, with Norfolk Yeomanry and Denbigh Yeomanry.

1/9/18: Bouchavesnes and Moislains: 74th Division reaches Canal du Nord defended by German Alpine Corps); 58th (London) Div. fails to secure Epehy on left (10/9/18) therefore 229th Brigade, which seized the St Emilie – Ronssoy objective, were driven off the ridge by enemy counter attack prior to retirement to the jumping-off line.

9/9/18: Brig. Gen. R. Hoare wounded by shell fire.

Appendix III

229th Brigade Action near Ramallah, 28 December 1917[1]

I am sorry to have missed the GOC today; I should have much liked to have shown him my battlefield, so that he could appreciate more fully the good work my gallant fellows have put in.

The attack on the west end of the Zeitun Ridge was comparatively easy, though it was a very stiff climb up, but it all went off without any hitch, though my fellows had to stick out a continuous shelling for many hours while waiting for the right of the 10th Division to get up somewhere near them – the advance being by the left, I felt bound to do this.

The second objective also presented no great difficulty, but the last objective of that evening, viz. the attack on the Kh. Shafa Hill, was a teaser. I think we got off cheaply because it was done in the dark, but the Turks had three tiers of sangars built, splendid cover, and many machine-guns, and it was pretty hot while it lasted.

We got shelled and sniped while drawing up orders and making preparations for the attack on Beitania.

After making a personal reconnaissance, I wiped out my original plan of first taking Beitania, and then swinging round to the north for P35 central, and made up my mind to go for Beitania, the village behind it, and P35 central simultaneously. And I was influenced in this decision by the knowledge that (1) My right flank was unprotected. (2) Beitania itself was untenable unless both the ridge beyond it and P35 central were also held. So I drew up the following plan – *vide* rough sketch.

Ayr & Lanark (Scots Fusiliers) on right, Fife & Forfar (Black Watch) on left to go for Beitania, but the right companies to push straight on without stopping at the village and make straight for the ridge.

As soon as that attack was started, Somersets, with two companies of Devons in support, to make for P35 central.

I kept the KSLI [King's Shropshire Light Infantry] in reserve behind the Kh. Shafa, and got twelve machine-guns into position, giving splendid covering fire to all attacking battalions, and "turned all the taps on" – they made a proper rattle.

I must point out that from Kh. Shafa to the village of Beitania is only about 1,000 yards on the map, but it entailed scrambling down off the top of a steep rocky hill, crossing a deep valley, and then another stiff ascent, all in the face of heavy machine-gun and rifle fire, while enemy guns did what they could to break up the attack.

But the men never hesitated and tore along as fast as they possibly could over the intervening 1,500 yards, and the whole business went with rare dash and go, and I really think we've brought off something like a "coup".

---

1   Composed by Brigadier-General Hoare for the edification of 74th Division headquarters, the minor operation described in this correspondence was, according to officially designated battle nomenclature, part of the 'Defence of Jerusalem' (26-30 December 1917). See Major C.H. Dudley Ward, *The 74th Yeomanry Division in Syria and France* (London: John Murray, 1922), pp. 146-48 and Major A.F. Becke, *Order of Battle Part 4: The Army Council, G.H.Q.s, Armies and Corps 1914-1918* (London: HMSO, 1945), p. 249.

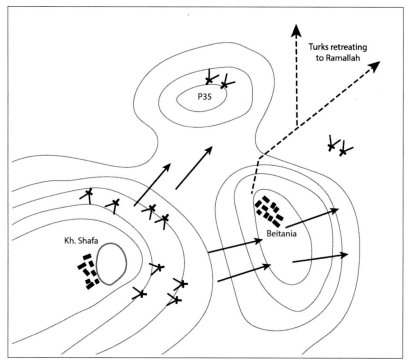

Jumping-off place Kh. Shafa

By attacking these three objectives simultaneously, I could only be subjected to a dispersed fire instead of a concentrated one, and on gaining my objectives, the Turks making away towards Ramallah came under a heavy crossfire of Lewis Guns from the three objectives gained and suffered severe losses. I don't reckon there is much left of the battalion, or whatever it was, holding the place – they were practically wiped out, and seven machine-guns is no small parcel to pick up in one stunt.

I am sure if you want to catch Turks, you must go at them fast, though it's not easy to go fast in this country.

The nature of the terrain of the operations makes it terribly difficult to find and bring in dead and wounded, as well as to find captured munitions of war, which are hidden among rocks.

Appendix IV

Correspondence from Major-General Eric Girdwood (GOC 74th Division)

My Dear Hoare,

Very many thanks for your two letters received yesterday and the day before. I cannot tell you how desperately sorry I am about your being wounded. I shall never forget all you have done for me and the loyal and unselfish way in which you have served under me when you might well have resented serving under such a junior officer. I thank you from the bottom of my heart for the many ways you have always helped me out. What I feel now is that I have temporarily lost a great friend.

They have already put a man in your place – one Thackeray HLI. I have only seen him from a few minutes on his arrival. I dare say he is a good man, but he can never make up to me for your loss. We are still having a busy time and great events loom ahead in the not far distance.

I hope to be able to give you all the news in my next letter. This is only a note until I know where you are.

I can imagine that you are very stiff and sore but the joys in store for you are some comfort and it is (provident the wounds are not serious) a splendid chance for you to get married and have a real rest.[1]

Let me know exactly what you propose to do as I want to write to people concerning your getting a Bgd at home until you are passed fit for G.S again. I shall urge for a Division, but I don't know what the Home list is like. Anyhow, old friend, you know that I'll do my very level best for you. The best of luck a quick recovery and all happiness to you. Love from all here and all my thanks again.

Yours Always
Eric Girdwood
18/9/18

---

1   RH asked (see letter 59) Girdwood to be his best man. In the event, the latter was unavailable, so Col. Cyril (Alers) Hankey, MVO stood in. He was the son of the great, great, great uncle of a Rupert Alers-Hankey whose wedding I officiated in the late 1990s.

Further Reading

Marquess of Anglesey, *A History of the British Cavalry Vol. 5, 1816-1919: Egypt, Palestine & Syria* (London: Leo Cooper, 1998).

Major A.F. Becke, *Order of Battle of Divisions Part 2A.: The Territorial Force Mounted Divisions and the 1st-Line Territorial Force Divisions (42-56)* (London: HMSO, 1936).

——*Order of Battle of Divisions Part 2B.: The 2nd Line Territorial Force Divisions (57th-69th) with the Home Service Divisions (71st-74th) and 74th and 75th Divisions* (London: HMSO, 1937).

David L. Bullock, *Allenby's War: Palestine Arabian Campaigns, 1916-18* (London: Weidenfeld, 1988).

Winston Churchill, *My Early Life* (London: Eland, 2000).

Rhys Crawley & Michael LoCicero, *Gallipoli: New Perspectives on the Mediterranean Expeditionary Force 1915-16* (Solihull: Helion & Company, 2018).

Major C.H. Dudley Ward, *The 74th Yeomanry Division in Syria and France* (London: John Murray, 1922).

Brigadier-General Sir J.E. Edmonds, *Military Operations France and Belgium 1918*, Vol. IV (London: HMSO, 1947).

Edward J. Erickson, *Palestine: The Ottoman Campaigns of 1914-1918* (Barnsley: Pen & Sword, 2016).

Captain Cyril Falls, *Military Operations Egypt and Palestine*, Vol. II, (London: HMSO, 1930).

W.G. Fisher, *The History of Somerset Yeomanry, Volunteer and Territorial Units* (Taunton: Goodman & Son, 1924).

Benson Freeman & Earl Fortescue, *The Yeomanry of Devon 1794-1927* (London: St Catherine Press, 1927).

Rob Johnson, *The Great War in the Middle East* (Oxford: Oxford University Press, 2016).

James E. Kitchen, *The British Imperial Army in the Middle East: Morale and Military Identity in the Sinai and Palestine Campaigns, 1916-18* (London: Bloomsbury, 2014).

Lieutenant-General Sir George MacMunn & Captain Cyril Falls, *Military Operations Egypt and Palestine*, Vol. I (London: HMSO, 1928).

Major D.D. Ogilvie, *The Fife and Forfar Yeomanry and 14th (F. & F. Yeo.) Battn. R.H. 1914-1919* (London: John Murray, 1921).

Robin Prior, *Gallipoli: The End of a Myth* (New Haven: Yale University Press, 2009).

Brig. Robin Rhoderick-Jones, *In Peace and War: The Story of The Queen's Royal Hussars (the Queen's Own and Royal Irish) Commissioned by Trustees of QRH* (Barnsley: Pen & Sword, 2018).

Brough Scott, *Churchill at the Gallop* (London: Racing Post, 2017).